For Bill Carl Martz

Contents

Introduction

The reader or spectator of Shakespearean comedy cannot help but marvel at how effective it is, how well it succeeds in making us laugh, and more. For this there is surely some fundamental reason. We observe in the comedies certain persistent qualities. Such qualities are, moreover, persistently absent in most of the alleged comedy to which we are exposed in our own day, the endless claptrap of television comedy being a general but epitomizing example. Why, then, does Shakespearean comedy succeed so well? The first reason is, I feel, that a "comic point of view" is established and, more important and more difficult, maintained. The second is that there is a distinct development of a "view of reality." But these reasons must be put together. Shakespearean comedy, viewed in broad outline, succeeds so well because it always shows a coincidence of a comic point of view and a development of a view of reality. The terms "comic point of view" and "view of reality" will, of course, have to be defined with care, but the vital emphasis would be lost if they were treated separately rather than in terms of how they coincide: how they constitute the overall dynamics of Shakespearean comedy. One gets an inkling of just how complicated the matter may become by merely thinking of such dynamics operative in a single play and then by a compounding process operative in a succession of plays. (There is, incidentally, no magic of dynamics in my selection and arrangement of the five plays to be discussed.) The compounding process is definitely not a matter of logically definable progression, the artist consciously creating a grand tableaux. Different comedies may actually be selected and viewed in a random order with the compounding process still taking place and proceeding toward the same end. The five plays, *The Taming of the Shrew*, *A Midsummer Night's Dream*, *As You Like It*, *Much Ado About Nothing*, and *Twelfth Night*, taken in the order which I have selected, essentially the order of composition, are, then, an illustration of the fundamental working, the dynamics of Shakespearean comedy, the final unity of which is distinctive in its kind and not a matter of formally definable patterns of progression.

Anchoring the present study is an assumption about norms and ethics in relation to the absurd or ridiculous. The absurd or ridiculous is simply not possible without norms or ethics. The very words themselves, *absurd* and *ridiculous*, represent value judgments, which can only be made in terms, by using standards of measurement. Such standards may, to be sure, be shifting or relative, but present they must be. As Bergson recognized, only human beings can be ridiculous. Comic point of view and view of reality as they will subsequently be defined both involve the assumption that the human thing being looked at and commented upon can only be looked at and commented upon in a world where value exists. Who can imagine the comic existing in an imaginary land of nihilism? I am reminded that Robert Frost "reveled" in using such devices as synecdoche; so does the comic dramatist revel in *his* devices, all to the end of affirmation. The comic dramatist believes in life. He has to. He revels in affirming life. He has to, because he could not create comedy apart from the very spirit of reveling. Thus we hint already at the coincidence between the comic point of view, here reveling, and a view of reality rationally held.

Comedy is the health of being human. Such health assumes norms to live by, provenance and roots, not to mention ethical convictions. Just as the comic cannot exist in an imaginary land of nihilism so, inversely, can the villain in comedy not exist in terms of the comic spirit's health. In ultimate philosophical terms the villain in comedy has nothing to live by, or for, but the mercy of the comic spirit often allows him a chance to reform, a chance to live more fully, perhaps to laugh at himself, perhaps even to revel.

To say that the absurd or ridiculous is not possible without norms or ethics prompts a statement on the relationship between comedy and tragedy as distinct art forms, for comedy can only exist in relationship to the kind of seriousness represented by tragedy. I would take this a step further and suggest that comedy should be seen steadily and distinctly in relationship to tragedy. Comedy is comedy because our fundamental consciousness of life involves what Paul Tillich in defining anxiety calls "awareness of one's own finitude." Such awareness is, I think, a necessary antecedent to laughter. We laugh if there is something to laugh at, or at least with. Laughter, it seems to me, often expresses what Tillich calls "the courage to affirm one's own being in terms of power and meaning in spite of the ever-present threat of non-being." Surely tragedy is graphic in its presentation of the possibility of non-being. No wonder, too, that we can laugh, and laugh very hard, within the framework of tragedy. How, then, shall we describe the relationship between

comedy and tragedy as distinct art forms? In my view
the most useful suggestion to this end is made by Maynard Mack in the introduction to his edition of *Joseph
Andrews.*

Mack focuses on the distinctive nature of the comic
point of view, comedy presenting us with "life appre-
hended in the form of spectacle rather than in the form
of experience." His reasoning proceeds from facts which
we all readily accept, that character in the tragic mode
"always inhabits . . . a world of choices followed by con-
sequences," that "the tragic emphasis seems to be on the
uniqueness and finality of human experience," that tragedy's curve of action is "a curve of self-discovery." He
finds the comic mode, on the other hand, emphasizing
"the permanence and typicality of human experience,
as projected in persistent social species whose sufficient
destiny is simply to go on revealing themselves to us."
He asks what to my mind is a most crucial question on
the relationship between comedy and tragedy as art
forms: where is, or what is the state of, our consciousness
as we view them? His answer is that in the tragic mode
the consciousness with which ours must be continuous
is the character's, whereas in the comic mode the consciousness with which our consciousness must be continuous is the author's. Thus in comedy we are aware
that we are sharing a comic point of view with the
author, whereas in tragedy we hardly find ourselves caring about the author's point of view, so interested do we
become in the tragic action in and of itself.

Comedy, as everyone knows, tends to prefer static
characters, types, whereas tragedy tends to prefer dynamic characters, individuals. In the following chapters

I shall be concerned to describe the relationship between Shakespeare's view of reality, a complex thing, and his use of characters suitable to comedy as an art form, for there is a limit to how simple the characters in comedy can be if a complex view of reality is to be developed, or, to put it another way and to modify Maynard Mack's view, character in comedy is not precluded from engaging our consciousness in a continuous way. I shall also present, following the separate treatment of each of the five plays in question, brief summaries of what for want of a better name must be called Shakespeare's theory of comedy. This theory will be inferred from the plays themselves and is, I think, an integral part of what they are saying. There is a distinct sense in which a theory of comedy is in fact each play itself, thence the plays themselves. A brief emphasis on theory will, I feel, suggest that Shakespeare knew what he was doing, that he was sure of his powers as early as 1593 and that his powers kept growing.

Ripon College
September, 1970

William J. Martz

Chapter One

"Comic Point of View"

There is a sense in which to try to define "comic point of view" is to try to define the indefinable. There is, as is generally agreed, no character in any Shakespearean play that can be rationally taken as Shakespeare himself or as Shakespeare's spokesman for his own views; in other words, Shakespeare is non-reductive and his genius as a dramatist is reflected in the fact that every character he creates has an individuality of his own and does not admit to being equated, in whole or in part, with his play's author. Point of view must, then, be inferred from a play's structure, from the observable facts of the playwright's virtually infinite number of choices creating a virtually infinite number of relationships that finally are the organic whole of the play itself. Such choices (whether conscious or unconscious) focus, of course, on such fundamentals of poetic drama's form as character, action, scene placement, diction, versification, and metaphor. We are openly aware of the effect which they create, which in comedy is usually, but not always, laughter. We may, however, only equate effect with author intent in a very general way, rather than with tight specificity. The problem of defining comic point of view thus becomes a problem of responding to structure as a representation of how the author feels toward life and how he sees life. His point of view, the totality of his attitude, must, ultimately, be as complex as the play itself. We face, as it were, two extremes, the total complexity of a given comedy on one side and on the other the rather obvious amusement that its creator would have to feel as one who has chosen to be so patently busy making us laugh or feel delight in the first place. Somewhere between these extremes we may find a descriptive definition of "comic point of view."

But before we examine to this end the five comedies selected for discussion, a further overview is necessary. I would like to suggest that comic point of view may be regarded as a frame. At the center of the frame is a square which must be called "farce." Farce, in turn, may be defined as extreme spectacle, the distance between the square of farce and the framing point of view being as great as it can be for comedy. Farce, which in elemental terms we know as the clown slipping on a banana peel, is a fundamental identification, a signpost, a norm for all comedy. Now imagine the square representing farce moving outward toward its distant frame. When it coincides with that frame, the comic point of view may be thought of as tending to dissolve, as no longer having a distinct identity, or as being transmuted into a serious point of view:

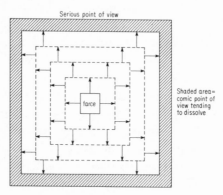

Where the arrows approach the shaded area in which comic point of view tends to dissolve we find *Twelfth Night*; in fact, some critics would actually place it within the shaded area, a position which I shall argue against. At the center of the diagram, for present purposes, is *The Taming of the Shrew*. The remaining three of our five are somewhere in between, but none of the plays should be thought of as assuming a static position in the diagram, for mature comedy is dynamic, and a farce such as *The Taming of the Shrew* radiates out toward the frame of serious point of view even though we always see it, as it were, at a distance, with the substantial detachment appropriate to a view of life as spectacle. Likewise, the darkest or most serious of the five comedies, *Twelfth Night*, moves inward toward farce though we never see it at the distance that typifies our view of *The Taming of the Shrew*. The framing point of view (which includes satire), if established and maintained, substantially defines what a particular comedy is and is not altered by the fact that it contains apparent opposites; for example, no matter how serious a theme *The Taming of the Shrew* develops, it remains a farce from first to last, and, similarly, no matter how farcical the incidents of *Twelfth Night* become it is not from first to last a farce.

I will, of course, explain this further in the separate chapters on the individual plays, but the work of the moment is a descriptive definition of comic point of view. Moreover, a better understanding of the nature of comedy will be achieved, I believe, if we look first at our five comedies together and then proceed to an analysis of them on an individual basis.

Shakespeare's basic problem in establishing a comic

point of view for *The Taming of the Shrew* may, I believe, best be seen by a focus on the character of Petruchio, for his character involves a crucial paradox with regard to the nature of comedy. He is a character of what I like to call *stature*, that is, the kind of character in whom we could easily take a serious interest, the kind of character with whose consciousness our consciousness could easily become continuous. If for the moment his stature may be accepted as a premise, the question becomes, why does Shakespeare put such a character into a farce? Is this not to run the risk of having the broad spectacle of farce turn into something contrary to its own nature? I am convinced that Shakespeare was cognizant of this problem, for it is of the utmost importance to what the play is that Shakespeare chose to hold the entrance of Petruchio until the beginning of the second scene of Act I. Were Petruchio to be the first person on the stage—without the Christopher Sly Induction—there would be great danger that he would so engage us that Shakespeare could hardly maintain the play as a farce at all.

If this is true, then the Induction and I, i must function to establish the play as a farce, to establish its framing point of view, as indeed they do. Christopher Sly is a "drunken man"—in effect a clown—on whom a funny joke is played, and part of the joke is that "you hear a play / And frame your mind to mirth and merriment" (Ind., ii, 136–37).[1] What such a character as Christopher Sly is expected to witness could hardly be expected to

[1] All citations of Shakespeare's plays in my text are from *The Complete Works of Shakespeare*, ed. Hardin Craig (Glenview, Ill.: Scott, Foresman, 1951).

be serious, not to mention tragic. The first scene of the play confirms our expectation. Baptista's first words define the condition that propels the entire plot:

> *Gentlemen, importune me no farther,*
> *For how I firmly am resolved you know;*
> *That is, not to bestow my youngest daughter*
> *Before I have a husband for the elder.*

(I, i, 48–51)

The rest of the scene establishes Kate as an unmarriageable shrew, particularly through comments of Hortensio and Gremio, who describe her as a devil, a fiend of hell. Scene i in effect calls for someone to tame Kate, and scene ii brings Petruchio to answer the call to accomplish that impossible task. Petruchio is thus placed within the framing point of view of scene i, which has no character of stature with the possible exception of Kate, who is held to a few lines. Furthermore, beautiful Bianca is clearly a cliché type, flat, personalityless, so we are scarcely involved at all with character until we meet Petruchio. When we do meet him, we meet with what I refer to above as a crucial paradox with regard to the nature of comedy, namely, that a character of stature can function in a rather statureless world (that is, a world not inhabited by other characters of stature) and not contradict that world despite the fact that essentially he does. The first reason why he does not contradict that world is that Shakespeare carefully establishes a framing point of view before introducing him. The second reason is that his development as a character is held within limits appropriate to the comic frame; a corollary to this second reason is the fact that he participates in action that we are invited to see as spectacle, namely, the farce incidents of the taming process, which Shakespeare carefully chooses to make the body of the play.

In sum, the comic point of view which Shakespeare establishes in *The Taming of the Shrew* is the mirth and merriment of the taming process. It might at this point be useful to recall *The Comedy of Errors*. In that play Shakespeare interests us in fact, that is, in a situation. In *The Taming of the Shrew*, by contrast, he interests us in process, in the quality of a situation. The move for him was a big one, and, as we know, he never returned to the relative mechanicalness of *The Comedy of Errors*. In *The Taming of the Shrew* process is spectacle rather than serious drama because, fundamentally, the gusto of Petruchio (and Kate) is placed within a comic frame and held to a succession of incidents within it. We thus have dramatic interest held at a distance, whereas in *The Comedy of Errors* we are at a distance but the dramatic interest is minimal. *The Taming of the Shrew* thus, to my way of thinking, begins to define mature Shakespearean comedy, strong dramatic interest within a well-established and well-maintained comic frame. This is not to say that as a play *The Taming of the Shrew* does not have structural problems. For example, why does Shakespeare choose to describe the dress and behavior of Petruchio at the wedding rather than to make the wedding into a scene, the sheer physicality of which we can enjoy? The basic answer is that he wishes to avoid boredom, which is a threat to this farcical a play. If Petruchio's behavior at his wedding to Kate were a scene, then the play would simply have too much repetition of the deprivation and humiliation of Kate. Farce by its nature—or we could say by definition—tends to minimize or to subdue both character and theme development.

Yet if character and theme development are overly minimized or overly subdued, the boredom of mere physical repetition or of all too slight variation is sure to result. A skit can only last so long. What makes *The Taming of the Shrew* a great play is not the thematic and character complexity we associate with, say, tragedy, but rather its magnificent balance. Shakespeare knew just how far to go, and just when to stop. Academic qualifications about the play's lack of complexity are irrelevant, for they focus on the wrong thing. It has its own kind of complexity, and the complexity, as we shall later see, is appropriate to what the play *is*. Farce, to put the matter a different way, is nothing to look down upon. In fact, to look down upon mature farce is to look down upon life.

That Shakespeare was fully aware that farce has something to do with the depth of our humanity is clear from the use which he makes of it in *A Midsummer Night's Dream*. Our description of comic point of view is, I think, best continued by observing what happens to farce in that play. I would posit that the play-within-the-play at the end of *A Midsummer Night's Dream* is more farcical than anything in *The Taming of the Shrew*. The rude mechanicals performing "The most lamentable comedy, and most cruel death of Pyramus and Thisby" are complete bumblers completely unaware of what they are doing. We see them at a distance and laugh at them as at that drunken clown Christopher Sly. And yet *A Midsummer Night's Dream* is not a farce. What, then, is its

framing point of view? We should first mention the purpose of the most farcical play-within-the-play performed
by the rude mechanicals. The purpose, Shakespeare's purpose, is to make us feel the quality of a paradox. The key
word is "translated," Quince's malapropism for "transformed." Shakespeare as author is saying, Here is a complete farce, the limit of ineptness, and yet I will present
it to you "translated" into a transcendent and transcendently funny act of the imagination. The paradox is that
the completely bad is sublimely good. Our consciousness
is thus not only very much with that of the author but
also controlled beyond the normal purposes of farce to
the point that we feel the deep beauty of the event, well
summarized in Theseus' sentimental aphorism, "For never
anything can be amiss, / When simpleness and duty
tender it" (V, i, 82–3). My assumption, of course, is that
farce normally does not seek to make us feel deeply. The
slip of the clown on a banana peel *cannot* lead to a broken
skull, cannot lead us to feel deeply, without being transmuted into something other than farce.

   Since the framing point of view is established at the beginning of a comedy, we should note that the rude mechanicals are introduced in the second scene of Act I
rather than in the first. Shakespeare was surely cognizant
of the fact that to introduce them first would be to arouse
in his audience an expectation of rollicking farce. So he
opens with Theseus and Hippolyta awaiting their nuptial hour and with the problems of the young lovers
Hermia, Lysander, Demetrius, and Helena. The character of Theseus is, it seems to me, the key to the comic
point of view which Shakespeare wishes to establish.
Theseus, moreover, invites comparison with Petruchio.
Petruchio behaves in a preposterous manner, but he

nevertheless has stature. Although we see him at a distance, we can nevertheless share his point of view and enjoy with him his own self-awareness. Theseus, as he exists within the framework of the play's action, is a character of stature, the eloquent and powerful Duke of Athens to whom others turn for law, for decisions. But this is not the way *we* see him. We see him rather as somewhat preposterous, not, certainly, as a creature of farce comedy, but as slightly absurd in his lack of the kind of self-awareness displayed by Petruchio. It is, for example, absurd of him to offer to Hermia the simple dichotomy of obedience, "or else":

> *For you, fair Hermia, look you arm yourself*
> *To fit your fancies to your father's will;*
> *Or else the law of Athens yields you up—*
> *Which by no means we may extenuate—*
> *To death, or to a vow of single life.*
>
> (I, i, 117–21)

We wonder whether or not he is a mechanist in the face of the law and we wonder, more largely, what manner of world could give rise to such simplistic notions as would lead Egeus to say of his daughter Hermia:

> *As she is mine I may dispose of her:*
> *Which shall be either to this gentleman*
> *Or to her death, according to our law*
>
> (I, i, 42–4)

Our perception of the absurdity of Theseus tends to be intellectual. Egeus may prompt an immediate laugh, but not Theseus, for despite his lack of self-awareness and

values questioning, Theseus has admirable personal qualities, warmth, sensitivity, tolerance, humanity. He does,
after all, offer Hermia the alternative of a cloister rather
than death, which in turn suggests his possible willing-
ness to let time solve the problem. But his ineptness to
handle the problem in any other way than the one he displays conditions us for the ineptness of the rude mechanicals in the following scene. In other words, it may not be
at all apparent, but the great Duke of Athens exists in
this relationship to the least of his subjects. If he had
hatred or contempt for them, we would be moving
toward satire, toward an exposure of a certain kind of
vicious reality which we know exists, the condemnation
of others for the very failures that we ourselves display.
But such is not the case. Instead we have the Theseus
who feels the deep beauty of nuptial anticipation giving
his order to his master of the revels: "Stir up the Athen-
ian youth to merriments; / Awake the pert and nimble
spirit of mirth" (I, i, 12–13). The spirit of mirth to
which Theseus refers suggests exuberance but not quite
the laughter-oriented "mirth and merriment" involved in
the taming of a shrew.

The young lovers in the first scene confirm the point
of view that Shakespeare is establishing through the character of Theseus. In their petulant youth and lack of
self-awareness they too are absurd. They differ from
Theseus, of course, in that their youth accounts for their
determined pursuit of their individual love interests. But
the fact that they have individual vigor is of the utmost
importance. Unlike Bianca, who distinctly lacks force of
personality, they attract our strong attention even though
we view them with considerable detachment. Not one of

them has the stature, the self-awareness and sheer interestingness, of either Petruchio or Kate, but each one does
have personal force, a will of his own. Lysander and
Hermia *choose* to leave Athens and to meet in the woods,
and Helena *chooses* to disclose this fact to Demetrius.
By the end of scene one we sense absurdity and our
curiosity has been aroused, but there is nothing comparable to the "set-up" of Baptista's decision not to allow
Bianca to marry until he finds a husband for Kate. The
comic point of view that Shakespeare establishes for
A Midsummer Night's Dream is, then, not the broad
spectacle of farce but rather a gently insinuated spectacle
of personal absurdity, with the spectator feeling a bemused and tolerant interest rather than being prompted
to laugh uproariously.

In the second scene we meet the rude mechanicals,
who also excite in us a bemused and tolerant interest; it
should be noted that this scene is essentially conversa-
tional, as if Shakespeare is choosing to mute the very possibility of the physicality typical of farce and its creatures.
The framing point of view for the play as a whole is
completed by the third scene (II, i), in which we meet
Puck, Oberon, and Titania. Oberon and Titania quarrel
absurdly over the changeling boy, Oberon exclaiming
after his wife leaves, "thou shalt not from this grove /
Till I torment thee for this injury" (II, i, 146–47). His
practical joke, to make use of the pansy juice that "Will
make or man or woman madly dote / Upon the next live
creature that it sees" (II, i, 171–72) propels the plot that
brings together Bottom and Titania and initiates a series
of identity confusions as he takes sympathy on Helena
and directs Puck to anoint the eyes of the disdainful youth

Demetrius. We view Oberon with bemused detachment mingled, perhaps, with some sympathy for him as a frustrated husband and with some admiration for his sympathetic concern for Helena; this detachment is, moreover, augmented by the fact, or convention, of his spirit identity in the fairy kingdom. Part of the humor of the scene is that Oberon is a sexually frustrated spirit, a husband disdained, since Titania has "forsworn his bed and company" (II, i, 62), but Shakespeare is careful not to give repeated and overt emphasis to this because such would be farce and possibly interfere with his concentration on character and relationship, the spectacle of personal absurdity which defines the comic point of view established by the end of the third scene. We are at a distance from the action of the play but not at as great a distance as with *The Taming of the Shrew*. Although not one of the characters we meet in *A Midsummer Night's Dream* has the force or magnetism of Petruchio, the world we are in has a quality of warmth, or warmly human relationship however imperfect, and of poetic beauty.

The key to the comic point of view of *As You Like It* is the character of Rosalind, for, as is widely agreed, this is Rosalind's play. In the light of the previous commentary it seems appropriate to compare her stature as a character with that of Petruchio or Theseus. She is, fundamentally, a character of great stature, a character with whose consciousness our consciousness may easily be continuous. As with Petruchio, Shakespeare holds her introduction into the play until the second scene, but his purpose in the first scene is not to establish a framing comic point of view to contain a character of her stature. Not only does *As You Like It* not even begin as a funny play, it hardly excites a laugh in the first two acts, either a laugh of the hearty type which we associate with *The Taming of the Shrew* or of the more bemused type of *A Midsummer Night's Dream*. The framing point of view in *As You Like It* is established slowly and does not emphasize laughter. What it emphasizes instead is probably best called the comic spirit, an attitude toward life that is fairly described as affirmative, romantic, idealistic.

With Rosalind we meet the Shakespearean heroine who embodies a whole set of such qualities, and this is why *As You Like It* is so much and so obviously her play. The first scene prepares us for her entrance by introducing her lover-to-be Orlando, but it is she who establishes the framing point of view. The problem that Shakespeare faces in introducing her is that he cannot let her dominate at once so greatly that incremental development of her character will be too difficult in comedy. She is essentially so interesting that she could if she developed from a strong beginning become so strong, so deeply engaging our consciousness continuously with hers, that she could move the whole point of view of the play outward to the shaded area of serious drama. For this reason Shakespeare develops her character gradually and she does not assume full stature until the full development of her relationship with Orlando in the middle and later part of the play. Unlike Theseus, who has great stature within the action of the play and opens that action, Rosalind at first is literally a bystander at a wrestling match.

Although it is perfectly obvious that she is falling in love with Orlando, our attention is not strongly directed to that fact. The fact of her love for him is, rather, sandwiched between the opening exchange between the two brothers and Oliver's discussion with Charles of the wrestling match (I, i) and the banishment shortly after the match of Rosalind by Duke Frederick (I, iii). With Petruchio we have early in the play a fairly full idea of what he is and then a hold on his development over the succession of farce incidents that constitute the taming process, but Rosalind, by contrast, is first presented in a low key. There is no character in *A Midsummer Night's Dream* that compares with Rosalind in stature as we come to see her, but it is important that the comic spirit of *A Midsummer Night's Dream*, its deep beauty apart from laughter, is akin to that of *As You Like It*. I do not, however, mean to imply that this spirit is absent in *The Taming of the Shrew*, for it is the nature of comedy to have this spirit, and the question is merely one of emphasis, a matter of balance between laughter and a spirit of affirmation, or a matter, perhaps, of the contrast between overt laughter, such as a guffaw, and being tickled inwardly.

In *Much Ado About Nothing* Shakespeare establishes a framing point of view by focusing on Beatrice and Benedick. As Leonato says,

> *There is a kind of merry war betwixt*
> *   Benedick and her:*
> *they never meet but there's a skirmish of wit*
> *   between them.*   (I, i, 61–3)

This skirmish of wit, with its persistent and pointed verbal play, begins with Beatrice's first words (I, i, 30) and continues to the very end of the play. It makes us laugh, and laugh heartily, but a central aspect of its ap-

peal is, of course, its intellectuality. When we think of
Beatrice and Benedick we think, in fact, of a downright
talky play. The physicality of farce is in their relationship conspicuous by its absence. They are—not surprisingly—characters of stature, highly aware of themselves
and of each other. They are what we call sophisticated people, and they like to joke and to communicate
in indirect ways. In broad terms they represent a refinement and a sophistication of the farcical wit of Petruchio
and Kate. Wit relates *The Taming of the Shrew* to
Much Ado About Nothing in a manner similar to the
way in which the comic spirit as delight in the deep
beauty of life relates *A Midsummer Night's Dream* to
As You Like It. As characters of stature Beatrice and
Benedick ostensibly compare with Rosalind, but they
do not actually approach her in fullness of stature and
in the centrality of her role in the world she inhabits. *As
You Like It* is Rosalind's play, but *Much Ado About
Nothing* is not Beatrice's and Benedick's play in anything
resembling the same sense. Why not? The answer is
Dogberry. In terms of the comic dramatist's handling of
character stature, *Much Ado About Nothing* is a divided
play. When Dogberry enters for the first time in III, iii,
he changes the whole play and dominates it. In light of
the comments I have made on stature, this may sound
strange, but the paradox is there. In terms of stature Dogberry resembles the rude mechanicals of *A Midsummer
Night's Dream.* He is uproariously funny as a complete
bumbler completely unaware of what he is doing. His
great tag line, "and masters, do not forget to specify,
when time and place shall serve, that I am an ass" (V, ii,
263–64), epitomizes him as a creature of farce. But, as

with the rude mechanicals, there is a sense—which comes as no surprise—in which he is "translated" into a perfect success as the man responsible for bringing the villain to justice. Thus the man least likely to bring justice does bring it, just as in *A Midsummer Night's Dream* the men least likely to show imagination show it in abundance.

But why would Shakespeare divide his play in the sense that I have suggested? Surely if he wished he would have the craft to work Dogberry into the action of the play without, as it were, pushing Beatrice and Benedick aside. A persuasive answer is that the wit of Beatrice and Benedick threatens to become tiresome over the entire length of the play, thus necessitating a shift to the farcical humor of Dogberry and his men. But a more fundamental reason is, I believe, that Dogberry as a character connects significantly to Beatrice and Benedick. Although an apparent opposite, he connects to them in spirit, for they are strongly individual, and so is he, and he is a creature beautiful in his innocence, and they are beautiful in the quality of their relationship, their love. But Shakespeare makes Dogberry even better—in a sense, of even greater stature—than Beatrice and Benedick, because Dogberry's love is universal, whereas theirs is more directed toward the end of their own marriage. Dogberry is utterly uncoercible, whereas Beatrice and Benedick end by cooperating with society even though their choice is strong to stand as individuals. Their love does not, of course, contradict universal love, but it is simply not as great. For Dogberry "it is an offence to stay a man against his will" (III, iii, 87-8); he perceives, that is, the deep beauty of freedom. Dogberry has, in fact, a universal sympathy and tolerance that is the hall-mark of the comic dramatist. But Shakespeare must by the nature of the case be like Beatrice and Benedick, a self-conscious intellectual. How, then, may he tran-scend the limitations of his own intellect and reach as far in spirit as his bumbling creation? The answer, I think, is that he *detaches* himself from his creation and lets its spirit of universal sympathy and tolerance imply that he offers it to us freely, offers it to us while, as it were, on his knees.

We approach *Twelfth Night*, then, with a sense that the comic spirit suggests an overall attitude of reverence for life, well expressed by an implied love for the least of God's creatures. It should be clear at this point that laughter has an intimate relationship to such an attitude and, furthermore, that laughter runs the gamut from the heartiest of guffaws to reflective interior smiles. But *Twelfth Night* is obviously different from the four com-edies which we have been discussing. It has a dark side, the formidable presence of which in a comedy is no small matter of puzzlement. The question can even be raised, Does it show a comic point of view or is it ac-tually a serious play? A good way to answer this ques-tion is to focus on the early scenes and to see if a framing point of view is established. Of crucial importance is that I, iii is so easily identified as farcical in intent. Sir Toby's last name is Belch, which Shakespeare does not have to deliver in the dialogue. Yet when Sir Andrew first enters he exclaims: "Sir Toby Belch! how now, Sir Toby Belch!" (I, i, 48). The name, of course, fits the man, as does Aguecheek for Sir Andrew, whom Toby announces as "Sir Andrew Agueface."

For Shakespeare to emphasize such name-jesting—not to mention that such clown figures are "Sir"—is for him to declare a farcical point of view, which in turn is confirmed by the jesting of Maria, Sir Toby, and Sir Andrew. The question becomes, then, do the first two scenes cooperate with this third scene to establish a framing point of view, or do the first two scenes, on the other hand, themselves establish the framing point of view, thus allowing farce to be framed by, for example, a serious point of view? The answer, I think, is the former, but the reason is perhaps not obvious. Duke Orsino is not a creature of farce and could be viewed as a romantic lover who might or might not propel a comedy. His mellifluous verse, in other words, might suggest a character with whose consciousness our consciousness could be continuous. There is a sense in which as a romantic lover he might be regarded as absurd, and another sense in which such a lover is not absurd at all. If the characterization is thus ambiguous, then it could not be said that a clear framing point of view is established, as we have maintained, for example, is the case with Theseus, whom *we* see as absurd even though he has stature within the action of the play.

But it is, I think, Shakespeare's intent that we do see Orsino as absurd and thus to be viewed in terms of life as spectacle or within the frame of a comic point of view. What we are invited to do is to measure him by our own linguistic norms, for the terms in which he speaks are excessive. Such norms are those which we carry to the play with us. Orsino, to put the matter another way, is just excessive enough in his speech to make us see him as an oddball and thus to view him at a distance. The artificial condition of Olivia's mourning, explained by

Valentine in response to Orsino's query about Olivia, confirms our suspicion that the play's intent is comedy, and it should also be noted that Valentine's speech resembles Orsino's own fancy love rhetoric:

> *The element itself, till seven years' heat,*
> *Shall not behold her face at ample view;*
> *But, like a cloistress, she will veiled walk*
> *And water once a day her chamber round*
> *With eye-offending brine: all this to season*
> *A brother's dead love*
>
> (I, i, 26–31)

The sophisticated viewer would, moreover, see at once the possibility that Olivia is simply using her brother's death as a ploy to fend off the suit of Orsino, and this in turn might evoke a hearty laugh. The second scene, between Viola and the Captain, confirms the comic point of view. The implication is clear that Viola will become romantically interested in Orsino and that her appearance in disguise at his court will lead eventually to their nuptials. We are thus viewing life as spectacle. Viola's key statement is a promise which takes the form of a double-entendre:

> *for I can sing*
> *And speak to him in many sorts of music*
> (I, ii, 57–8)

The context suggests that Viola's meaning is chiefly literal, but Shakespeare's clear intent is to suggest that her promise is the rhythm of sexual contentment, and thus we are viewing Viola through the filtering medium of his author consciousness. The spirit informing the remark, both Viola's spirit and the author's, is one of affirmation, and it may be directly compared with Rosalind's promise to Orlando as she speaks to him with toying good humor while still in the disguise she is about to abandon:

> *I will satisfy you, if ever I satisfied man,*
> *and you shall be married to-morrow.*
>
> (V, ii, 123–24)

Her promise is a joyous one of the sexual contentment of marriage. At the time Viola makes her promise she has, of course, not even met Orsino; it is thus as if Shakespeare is wryly making the promise for her. The first two scenes of *Twelfth Night* thus begin to frame a comic point of view which the third scene confirms and complements through its farcical quality. *Twelfth Night* is thus, I think, distinctly a comedy rather than something else. The gulling of Malvolio is, moreover, extremely farcical; we may note, for example, that Malvolio is "set up" in terms of his own vanity in a substantial scene (65 lines) just before in II, v he finds the letter which he takes to be from Olivia. Shakespeare's handling of Malvolio suggests that he definitely wanted to maintain the point of view initiated in the first three scenes. In a later chapter, I shall discuss how the dark side of *Twelfth Night* relates to and is held within this framing point of view.

We should now think of "comic point of view" as the totality of author attitude which can be inferred from the structure of the play which we designate a comedy; or, we could as easily say that when a definite author attitude is perceived (and eventually is total) we may then designate a play as a comedy. But we must specify what is definite about the attitude perceived. What, most broadly, is definite is what I have referred to as "the comic spirit," or, to avoid the appearance of circular definition, we could simply say an affirmative spirit, one that encourages us to feel delight, or a deep beauty in life, or perhaps even a reverence for life. Concomitant with this spirit will usually be laughter, which in turn ranges from hearty guffaws to interior smiles. Comedy should not be thought of as merely that which excites laughter *unless* laughter is construed in a complex psychological way, as a kind of total reaction to life and one which does not necessarily involve what we *hear* as a laugh. "Comic point of view" as the totality of author attitude inferred from structure also involves the idea of a frame, a distinct view of life as spectacle, a distance from, a detachment from, what we are viewing. The idea of a framing point of view involves in turn the question of what is framed and why, which immediately necessitates a focus on character.

Character in comedy has to be appropriate to what comedy is, that is, not of such overwhelming stature that we no longer can feel the comic point of view of the author but are rather led to feel directly with the character, as we do in tragedy. A character of stature is one who displays deep self-awareness and also exercises choice, as opposed to being a mere puppet of the play's author. So a key question of comedy is the *degree* of stature a given character has and for that particular comedy, why. Paradox, however, comes into play, in that that comedy may itself involve or be a treatment of the an apparently statureless character may actually have great stature. It can hardly be emphasized too strongly that comedy must involve the dynamics of character although limits are imposed on character development. We might be prompted to ask how free a given character is, and how controlled by the author. This in turn suggests dynamics of freedom. As we move from comedy to comedy we may, moreover, perceive that comedy is not really based on a flat yes or no with regard to the question of personal freedom but is concerned, rather, to present the dynamics of such freedom to us as a mystery.

Chapter Two

"View of Reality"

If "comic point of view" may be defined as the totality of author attitude which can be inferred from the structure of the play which we designate a comedy, then "view of reality" is probably best defined as the totality of author *idea* which can be inferred from the structure of the play being considered. This in turn involves the assumption that there is a distinct sense in which a play is an organization of ideas, or as we commonly say, of themes. Although it is of limited value to try to reduce a complex play to a single statement of theme, we know (going as far back as Aristotle) that it is particularly important to see a play in terms of its own internal necessity, the *end* toward which it proceeds and which is meaningful only in terms of what has preceded it. We are, as it were, forced in the direction of rationally summarizable thematic content while conscious of the fact that such content may always be expressed in a variety of ways. What is really important, of course, is not the thematic content or the particular expression of it which a given critic may conclude upon but rather the description of the whys and wherefors of the play's structure that have led to a given set of conclusions. Just as we value the experience of the play in some ultimate sense, so do we value the experience of criticism as it functions to open to us a fuller experience of the play than we might otherwise have. The reason why we are uncomfortable in the presence of theme statements which *ap-*

pear reductive is that we feel a strong tension between reductive simplicity and experiential complexity. There is no easy way to relieve such tension but we should try to keep discussion of idea or theme in a larger perspective that relates to the nature of an art form. In terms of the present discussion we may ask what ideas or themes the comic point of view frames and why they cooperate with the comic frame, that is, what there is about them that complements rather than contradicts the comic dramatist's purposes, and in this way we may be able to suggest the nature of the coincidence between comic point of view and view of reality that is a chief characteristic of really good comedy and particularly of mature Shakespearean comedy.

What *The Taming of the Shrew* taken as a whole "means," what the play is "saying," may be expressed in a simple paradox involving the relationship between appearance and reality: The apparent shrew (Kate) is not actually a shrew at all but will be, rather, a good wife, whereas the apparent ideal—or at least idol—girl (Bianca, Italian for white) will be a shrew of a wife. The last scene of the play makes this theme quite explicit:

> Baptista: *Now, in good sadness, son Petruchio,*
> *I think thou hast the veriest shrew of all.*
> Petruchio: *Well, I say no: and therefore for*
>   *assurance*
> *Let's each one send unto his wife;*
> *And he whose wife is most obedient*
> *To come at first when he doth send for her,*
> *Shall win the wager which we will propose.*
>   (V, ii, 63–9)

Kate, of course, answers the summons, whereas Bianca, now Lucentio's wife, and Hortensio's wife, do not. Bianca, in turn, reveals herself as a shrew in her comment to Lucentio as he complains of losing one hundred crowns on her account: "The more fool you, for laying on my duty" (V, ii, 129). But matters are not, I think, quite as formulaic and superficial as they might seem, for Bianca, exchanging "a bitter jest or two" with Petruchio just before the wager, says to Petruchio:

> *Am I your bird? I mean to shift my bush;*
> *And then pursue me as you draw your bow.*
> (V, ii, 46–7)

Bianca's jest is bawdy. Her "bush" is her female sexual organ, which she will shift according to what she regards as the expediency of her personal security. Her husband, in other words, will be sexually tormented, or bribed. She is mocking Petruchio as the kind of husband who could not dominate her sexually, her concept of marriage being, of course, one that accepts sexual dominance by one partner or the other. The ideal of a free self freely given in marriage, a union of spirit between man and woman, is not for her. Petruchio, who loves Bianca's humor but does not share her cynicism, drinks "a health to all that shot and miss'd" (V, ii, 51), that is, to all men who in a high state of sexual excitement pursued such women as Bianca and ejaculated before they could catch up with them. That Shakespeare intends this emphasis for those who can catch it is confirmed in the dialogue shortly following:

> Baptista: *Son, I'll be your half, Bianca comes.*
> Lucentio: *I'll have no halves; I'll bear it all my-*
> *self.*
>
> Re-enter Biondello
> *How now! what news!*
> Biondello: *Sir, my mistress sends you word*
> *That she is busy and she cannot come!*
> Petruchio: *How, she is busy and she cannot come!*
> *Is that an answer?* (V, 178–83)

Petruchio, as from the beginning of the play, loves the bawdy jest. He sees that Bianca cannot "come" to a sexual climax because she simply does not have real interest in sex, and he wonders, moreover, how she could be "busy" concentrating on sex and still not come to a climax. One could, in fact, easily argue that Shakespeare intends to suggest that Bianca is frigid. Baptista's remark refers, of course, merely to the possibility of Bianca answering the call of her husband to make an appearance as a sign of wifely duty. Lucentio's "I'll bear it all myself" refers ostensibly to the wager but in the context of Petruchio's remark takes on the ironic meaning that he will indeed have the misery of being married to Bianca to bear all himself. Lucentio, though *he* does not know it and *we* do, cannot look forward to a marriage that will include sexual contentment. Bianca thus emerges at the end of the play as a frigid shrew, or at least as a wife who will use sex in order to dominate her husband. For her, marriage will not be true relationship. For Kate it will be, and the last scene must also make this clear so that we will see the extreme contrast contained in the paradox that Kate is not actually a shrew but will be a good wife and that Bianca is not actually a good wife but will be a shrew.

At the very end of the play Petruchio turns to Kate and directs her to tell the women present "What duty they do owe their lords and husbands" (V, ii, 131). Kate responds with a forty-three line speech which is a parody of Petruchio's hyperbolic humor and thus suggests their union of spirit. At Petruchio's direction Kate directs her first words at the Widow (who has recognized that he is "mocking"):

> *Fie, fie! unknit that threatening unkind brow,*
> *And dart not scornful glances from those eyes,*
> *To wound thy lord, thy king, thy governor.*
> (V, ii, 136–39)

And a moment later Kate repeats the hyperbolic pattern in defining a husband:

> *Thy husband is thy lord, thy life, thy keeper,*
> *Thy head, thy sovereign;* (V, ii, 146–47)

Kate thus joins Petruchio in mocking the Widow and the other ladies present. She also throws in a qualifying phrase that the others will not notice but that Petruchio surely will:

> *And when she is froward, peevish, sullen, sour,*
> *And not obedient to his honest will,*
> *What is she but a foul contending rebel*
> *And graceless traitor to her loving lord?*
> (V, ii, 157–60)

What precisely does she mean, we wonder, by "his honest will"? Is she not subtly enjoining him to a high standard of conduct in their relationship, accepting the rhetoric of obedience while insisting on the reality of a relationship of true exchange, of equality? She herself, moreover, plays the game of mocking the world's rhetoric by seeming to accept it, as a moment later she says,

> *Why are our bodies soft and weak and smooth,*
> *Unapt to toil and trouble in the world,*
> *But that our soft conditions and our hearts*
> *Should well agree with our external parts?*
>
> (V, ii, 165–68)

There is nothing in the play to suggest that she *believes* this cliché image of the delicate female. What she believes is that women have the quality we often call femininity. Of course she will use her feminine wiles to twist Petruchio to her ways, and Petruchio will understand what she is doing and make his adjustments accordingly. This is a far different thing from Bianca's concept of sexual torment and bribery, for Bianca is expressing a cold attitude toward life, whereas Kate is accepting the conditions of a delightful game. At the end of her speech Petruchio is well pleased with what she has said, "Why, there's a wench! Come on, and kiss me, Kate" (V, ii, 180). When he calls her a wench he is telling her that he understands what she is saying, that is, the difference between what she seems to be saying and what she actually means. The others do not understand. Shakespeare thus ends the play with a perfect last line, as

Lucentio says, "'Tis a wonder, by your leave, she will be tamed so."

The word *imagination* is not used once in *The Taming of the Shrew*. Yet the theme of the play may be summarized as a meaningful relationship between the sexes is an act of the imagination. Petruchio and Kate embody this imagination and stand in strong contrast to Bianca and her suitors. The imagination of true communication between the sexes is, moreover, characterized by the game they play, which is a game designed both to be communication and to make real communication possible. Imagination, a value in itself, relates by implication to other values, for the characters who show us imagination also have the best values, values that spell a chance for enduring happiness. Petruchio and Kate revel in human life and its possibilities. They laugh while they enjoy life. For them sex without humor is but a shadow of a meaningful relationship. Shakespeare, as comic dramatist, thus creates for us a universe of comedy, a world where the human spirit affirms itself and where values are there to make affirmation possible.

As with *The Taming of the Shrew* what *A Midsummer Night's Dream* taken as a whole "means," what the play is "saying," may be expressed in a simple paradox involving the relationship between appearance and reality: the life of the imagination (reality) is more real than any literal reality (appearance). Shakespeare with great deliberateness presents to us a "dream," and yet that dream is an experience so real as to make everyday reality seem by contrast like a rather meaningless appearance. His subject in the play is the relationship between life and art, with art becoming the sine qua non of a meaningful life. Recall Julius Caesar saying of Cassius, "he loves no plays . . . he hears no music" (I, ii, 203–04). At the root of Shakespeare's treatment of the subject is the very nature of dramatic art. It is a representation of reality rather than what we usually think of as reality itself. We walk into a theatre to see a play to "get away from" the reality outside. There is a sense in which, as Samuel Johnson in his *Preface to Shakespeare* well recognized, we always know that we are simply in a theatre watching a play: "The truth is, that the spectators are always in their senses, and know, from the first act to the last, that the stage is only a stage, and that the players are only players." This experience is thus by definition somewhat artificial and yet, paradoxically, more real than whatever is going on outside the theatre.

Shakespeare in *A Midsummer Night's Dream* is enacting for us a justification of the necessity of the experience of art to a meaningful life. It is as if he presents himself, wryly, with a tremendous challenge, to create in his play an imaginative reality so persuasive that when the play is over the spectator must affirm, consciously or unconsciously, the truth of the reality upon which the playwright and the play are insisting. It is as if Shakespeare were to say to the spectator, I will show you by my art the experience of the imagination and you will affirm by your experience of the play the truth of what I am saying. Metaphorically speaking, *A Midsummer Night's Dream* invites us to test the perception of our senses and ask, with Christopher Sly:

> *Am I a lord? and have I such a lady?*
> *Or do I dream? or have I dream'd till now?*

I do not sleep: I see, I hear, I speak;
I smell sweet savours and I feel soft things.

(Ind. ii, 70–3)

And then, like Sly, to affirm, "Upon my life, I am a
lord indeed." At the end of *A Midsummer Night's
Dream* the fact of the imagination is affirmed, as if the
spectator were to say, "Upon my life, I have indeed
experienced this truth." Or we may recall another statement in Johnson's *Preface to Shakespeare.* Having emphasized that it is false to mistake any representation for
reality, Johnson writes, "The objection arising from
the impossibility of passing the first hour at *Alexandria,*
and the next at *Rome,* supposes that when the play opens
the spectator really imagines himself at *Alexandria,* and
believes that his walk to the theatre has been a voyage to
Egypt, and that he lives in the days of *Antony* and *Cleo-
patra.*" Johnson then adds, in what surely is intended as
a wry comment, "Surely he that imagines this, may imagine more." Shakespeare in *A Midsummer Night's Dream*
in effect takes the "more" and shapes it into an experiential reality that we do not mistake for something else
but rather whose truth we affirm.

The subject of *The Taming of the Shrew* is the relation of the sexes. *A Midsummer Night's Dream* involves
us strongly in the relation of the sexes, but its subject is
the imagination, or the relationship between art and life.
In the first scene of Act III we find the rude mechanicals
making the same fundamental mistake to which Johnson
is objecting in his *Preface.* Their subject is the relationship between a representation of reality and reality itself:

Starveling: *I believe we must leave the killing out, when all is done.*

Bottom: *Not a whit: I have a device to make all well. Write me a prologue; and let the prologue seem to say, we will do no harm with our swords and that Pyramus is not killed indeed; and, for the more better assurance, tell them that I Pyramus am not Pyramus, but Bottom the weaver: this will put them out of fear.*

(III, i, 15–23)

Bottom assumes that his audience will mistake his representation of Pyramus for reality. His solution is simple: tell them that the representation is not in fact a reality. In his ignorance Bottom is unable to grasp the idea that the spectators are always in their senses and, of course, we know that his acting will be so bad that no one could possibly mistake it for reality, that is, that the confusion between representation and reality which he posits could only occur or even be thought of as occurring if his acting were superb. His acting will, however, *be* superb, as the totally bad play-within-the-play turns out to be sublimely good, a sublimely good representation, that is, of the supreme power of the imagination. There is thus an important sense in which he speaks the truth when he says, "I have a device to make all well." What he means, without knowing it, is that he has the dramatist's art. Shakespeare is, after all, backing him to the hilt.

When Bottom, having been released by Puck from the spell which put as ass's head on him, awakes from his "dream," his first reference is to the play, as if Shakespeare is linking the dramatist's art with the idea of a dream and thus hinting that reality is problematic, that although we are always in our senses as we watch a play, nevertheless our senses are short of final:

> *When my cue comes, call me, and I will answer: my next is, 'Most fair Pyramus,' Heigh-ho! Peter Quince! Flute, the bellows-mender! Snout, the tinker! Starveling! God's my life, stolen hence and left me asleep!*

Bottom then makes what is probably the best statement of the theme of *A Midsummer Night's Dream*:

> *I have had a most rare vision. I have had a dream, past the wit of man to say what dream it was: man is but an ass, if he go about to expound this dream. Methought I was—there is no man can tell me what. Methought I was—and methought I had,—but man is but a patched fool, if he will offer to say what methought I had. The eye of man hath not heard, the ear of man hath not seen, man's hand is not able to taste, his tongue to conceive, nor his heart to report, what my dream was.*
>
> (IV, i, 204–17)

The dream, then, is a *vision*, a moment of, a perception of something beyond one's own finitude, a mystical assurance, perhaps, that man does indeed have being. Clearly reason, the power "to expound" cannot touch it, and so transcendent is it that the eye of man cannot hear it, that is, our chief sense, transcending itself, cannot transcend itself to that extent. And yet *A Midsummer Night's Dream*, taken as a whole, is such a vision, and we read it, or watch it, as that or at least as a waking dream. I often think that when Shakespeare wrote it, at approximately the age of thirty, it must have been humility's own shakedown for him to have to admit to himself that he had such talent.

What *As You Like It* taken as a whole "means," what the play is "saying," is well summarized in Harold Goddard's apt phrase, "imaginative love," which "takes its cue from the arts, of which it is one and perhaps the highest." Taking our own cue from *A Midsummer Night's Dream* we could add that imaginative love involves two people having, at levels appropriate to their individual personalities, a "rare vision" of each other, a glimpse of true being in a certain kind of experiential reality. In *As You Like It* this imaginative love is first Rosalind's simple device—she has a device to make all well—to have Orlando woo her thinking that she is the boy Ganymede pretending to be Rosalind. The love between them, again as Goddard so aptly puts it, "is rehearsed in the kingdom of the imagination, where all true love begins." This love rehearsal in the kingdom of the imagination, which gets underway in III, ii, is the dramatic heart of the play, and the articulate Rosalind readily describes her experience of imaginative love, as, for example, in this comment to her cousin Celia a moment after Orlando has departed:

> O *coz, coz, coz, my pretty little coz, that thou didst know how many fathom deep I am in love! But it cannot be sounded: my affection*

hath an unknown bottom, like the bay of Portugal.

(IV, i, 209–12)

This is thematically parallel to Bottom's comment at the end of his awaking speech when he says, "I will get Peter Quince to write a ballad of this dream: it shall be called Bottom's Dream, because it hath no bottom" (IV, i, 217–20). The ear of man cannot see the bottom of the bay of Portugal. Imaginative love is a perception of something beyond one's own finitude.

I have previously suggested that the comic spirit of *A Midsummer Night's Dream*, its deep beauty apart from laughter, is akin to that of *As You Like It*. It is easy to see and easy to say that the theme of the imagination links the two plays, but are we not in fact saying that the theme of the imagination can hardly be separated from the quality with which it is presented in the two plays? In other words, if we were to emphasize a strictly thematic connection between *A Midsummer Night's Dream* and *As You Like It* we would depend on such words as *imagination* and *vision* at least to imply a certain attitude toward life. In point of fact *As You Like It* connects in a strictly thematic sense more closely with *The Taming of the Shrew* than with *A Midsummer Night's Dream*, for the subject of *The Taming of the Shrew* and of *As You Like It* is the relationship between the sexes and the essential conclusion which both plays reach about the relationship is the same, namely, that a meaningful relationship between the sexes is an act of the imagination. Both plays, moreover, are concerned to demonstrate their truth, *The Taming of the Shrew*

through the taming process and *As You Like It* through
the love rehearsal in the kingdom of the imagination, or
Rosalind's magic, since she has "conversed with a magician, most profound in his art" (V, ii, 68–9)—no doubt
the wry Shakespeare.

It would hardly be going too far to say that Rosalind
is taming or educating Orlando and Petruchio and Kate
are experiencing a love rehearsal in the kingdom of the
imagination through the succession of episodes that constitute the taming process. To put the matter another
way, both plays conceive of the relationship between the
sexes as a game and show us how the game works. They
thus take a similar view of reality and combine it, of
course, with a spirit of affirmation, and yet when it
comes to a final decision of emphasis *As You Like It*
gravitates toward *A Midsummer Night's Dream* in the
quality of its view of life and we could at this point say
the quality of its theme. Or, to take a somewhat formulaic approach to the matter of Shakespeare's development
as a comic dramatist, we could say that he combines his
essential theme of the relationship between the sexes in
The Taming of the Shrew with his essential view of
life as a thing of "dream" in *A Midsummer Night's
Dream* and the result is *As You Like It*.

What *Much Ado About Nothing* taken as a whole
"means," what it is "saying," is more difficult to summarize than the same for *The Taming of the Shrew*, *A
Midsummer Night's Dream*, and *As You Like It*. In the
previous chapter I suggested that in broad terms Beatrice
and Benedick represent a refinement and a sophistication
of the farcical wit of Petruchio and Kate, which in turn
raises the question of whether or not the theme of *Much
Ado About Nothing* may not simply be that a meaning-

ful relationship between the sexes is an act of the imagination. Or, following *As You Like It*, we could ask if
Beatrice and Benedick continue the idea of the love rehearsal in the kingdom of the imagination. Clearly the
answer to both of these questions is affirmative. Beatrice
and Benedick do represent a certain perfection of the
imagination in the relationship between the sexes and
they do play the game of "wooing" throughout the play
even though they are "victims" of a charming joke designed to bring them together and to get them to express
what they obviously feel anyway. We might also profit-
ably compare the theme of *A Midsummer Night's
Dream* with *Much Ado About Nothing*.

I have suggested that the theme of *A Midsummer
Night's Dream* may be expressed this way: the life of
the imagination is more real than any literal reality. This,
it seems to me, is clearly not the main thematic emphasis
of *Much Ado About Nothing*, though it is present in
the play and is a true but partial description of the relationship of Beatrice and Benedick, who generally represent the triumph of true love typical of comedy, the in-
evitable "happy ending." In sum, Shakespeare takes the
essential theme of the relationship between the sexes from
The Taming of the Shrew and reshapes it for *Much Ado
About Nothing*, but he does not take the essential view
of life as a thing of "dream" from *A Midsummer Night's
Dream* and transfer it to *Much Ado About Nothing* as
he did with *As You Like It*. To approach *Much Ado
About Nothing* is in a very significant sense to abandon
the world of "dream" and even the quality of the imaginative triumph of Petruchio and Kate. The farcical
earthiness (or earthy farcicality) of *The Taming of the
Shrew* does not come through forcefully as a metaphor

of dream or vision, but the gusto of Petruchio and Kate implies transcendence or a perception of something beyond one's own earthiness. When we come to *Much Ado About Nothing* gusto gives way to intellect. The healthy animal nature of Petruchio and Kate is, in part at least, replaced by what today we usually call "anxiety." I do not mean to say that Beatrice and Benedick are nervous wrecks, but their intellectual intensity distinctly implies inner tension, and in the world they inhabit it is difficult for imagination to realize clear-cut triumphs. Or, to put the matter another way, the social order, which is internalized by the intellect, comes into conflict with the happiness of the individual. The happiness promised to Petruchio and Kate and to Rosalind and Orlando is, it seems to me, unlimited, as is the power of the imagination in *A Midsummer Night's Dream*. But *Much Ado About Nothing*, though it beautifully affirms, is strongly concerned with limits.

What *Much Ado About Nothing* means, what it is saying, is well summarized by Benedick at the very end of the play:

> *In brief, since I do purpose to marry, I will*
> *think nothing to any purpose that the world*
> *can say against it;*   (V, iv, 105–07)

A man must, that is, create his own world of value. Benedick has just discovered that he can't write a sonnet and thus he rejects conventions that are false anyway:

> *Marry, I cannot show it in rhyme; I have*
> *tried: I can find out no rhyme to 'lady' but*

> *'baby,' an innocent rhyme; for 'scorn,' 'horn,' a*
> *hard rhyme; for 'school,' 'fool,' a babbling*
> *rhyme; very ominous endings: no, I was not*
> *born under a rhyming planet, nor I cannot woo*
> *in festival terms.* (V, ii, 35–41)

Although Benedick here is affirming his individuality, he is also, without realizing it, poignantly revealing to us his own limitation. Had he been born under a rhyming planet, he might be able to sing beyond intellect. Were he able to woo in festival terms, that is, for the pure delight of it, his life might be unqualifiedly joyous, as Rosalind's promises to be. Instead he and Beatrice end as both free and compromised. They will assert their wills for freedom, but its achievement is far from guaranteed. Early in the play at the masked ball Beatrice, hearing the music struck up, says to Benedick, "We must follow the leaders." Benedick replies with a clear insistence that following be a values choice: "In every good thing." Beatrice then replies with a variant to his theme: "Nay, if they lead to any ill, I will leave them at the next turning" (II, i, 156–60). But this is essentially ethical discussion rather than a song of joy between them.

Nor is the function of Dogberry in the play to "translate" it into affirmation unlimited. Although Dogberry, as I have suggested, shows universal love and is beautiful in his innocence, his part in the action of the play is subordinate to the problems of the lovers. He enters in Act III, scene iii, and exits in Act V, scene i. He is not on stage at all in the first scene of Act IV, a scene of some 338 lines, whereas when he is on stage in the second scene of Act IV, the scene is only some 89 lines long. Quantity is of course neither proof nor argument but surely this suggests that it is not Shakespeare's intent to have him dominate the play and turn it into universal love as a form of comedy's affirmation unlimited. His function, rather, is to define by contrast with his own limitless freedom the limits of the world which Shakespeare calls Messina.

To turn to *Twelfth Night* is at this point to be prompted to suggest that the five plays under discussion fall into two groups, the first consisting of *The Taming of the Shrew*, *A Midsummer Night's Dream*, and *As You Like It*, the second of *Much Ado About Nothing* and *Twelfth Night*. For like *Much Ado About Nothing*, *Twelfth Night* affirms but is strongly concerned with limits. It is not a comedy that sings beyond intellect. In fact, I would go as far as to say that it creates a world of anti-dream, and thus is a perfect balance to the "dream" world of *A Midsummer Night's Dream*. In *Twelfth Night*, as in *Much Ado About Nothing*, the social order, which is internalized by the intellect or as part of the total personality, comes into conflict with the happiness of the individual. If in *Much Ado About Nothing* the healthy animal nature of Petruchio and Kate is in part replaced by what today we usually call "anxiety," then in *Twelfth Night* that healthy animal nature is replaced by what we would probably call neurosis, despite the fact, or rather complementing the fact, that animal nature is one of *Twelfth Night*'s most distinguishing characteristics.

What *Tweflth Night* taken as a whole "means" or is "saying" is much more difficult to summarize than for the four other plays under discussion but is, I think, possible. The subject of *Twelfth Night* is clearly not the con-

ventional one of the relationship between the sexes, but
rather, as with *Much Ado About Nothing*, the relationship of the individual to a world of value or to values
choices. It concludes, of course, with the happy ending
typical of comedy and thus with the affirmation of the
possibility of human happiness, but its thematic (and we
must also say tonal) emphasis is not on the triumph of
true love or the perfect experience of imaginative love,
not that is, on happiness unlimited, but rather on happiness as a condition of compromise. Just as in *Much Ado
About Nothing* Shakespeare defines the limits of the
world which he calls Messina, so does he in *Twelfth
Night* define the limits of the world which he calls
Illyria.

The only character in *Twelfth Night* who could in
terms of stature follow affirmatively on the heels of Petruchio, Bottom, Rosalind, Beatrice, Benedick, and
Dogberry is Sir Toby, but Sir Toby is not in their tradition, for despite his energy his value is patently excess. He
is "a drowned man," as the Clown says (I, v, 139) and,
as Olivia confirms, "he's in the third degree of drink, he's
drowned" (I, v, 143–44). When Bottom says that he
has a device to make all well, he is, as it were, reaching
for the stars, but when Maria tells Sir Toby of her
scheme to dupe Malvolio by dropping in his way "some
obscure epistles of love," Sir Toby's reply, "Excellent!
I smell a device" (II, iii, 176), is by contrast an image of
an earthly sniffer, of a man who is more like a hound
than a reacher for the stars. Sir Toby's use of the word
device is an act of gloating, whereas Bottom does not
even know how to gloat. Nor is the gulling of Malvolio
directed, as Dogberry's whole being is directed, toward

universal justice, for Malvolio is in no sense a villain and in no sense comparable to Don John. Bottom says, "I have had a dream, past the wit of man to say what dream it was." Sir Toby, reveling in Malvolio's discomfort, says, "Why, thou hast put him in such a dream, that when the image of it leaves him he must run mad" (II, v, 211–12). Clearly the concept of "dream" has altered radically as we move from the one play to the other. Bottom's dream is a marvelously fruitful one. Sir Toby, by contrast, engages in what Olivia with insight calls "fruitless pranks" (IV, i, 59). At the end of *Twelfth Night* when we learn that Sir Toby has married Maria, we can only wonder what kind of compromise, what kind of anti-dream, their lives together will be.

The contrast between *A Midsummer Night's Dream* and *Twelfth Night*, between "dream" and "anti-dream," or more largely the contrast of groups, the first three plays discussed and the last two, suggests that the view of reality taken by a given comedy may well represent the playwright's choice to move in one of two basic directions, either toward affirmation that is virtually unlimited (as an act of faith is virtually unlimited) or toward affirmation that is clearly a thing of limits (as the life we know constantly is). What *determines* this direction is clearly not the kind of humor involved, such as farce or wit. Both *The Taming of the Shrew* and *Twelfth Night* are, for example, extremely farcical, but *The Taming of the Shrew* is saying that a meaningful relationship between the sexes is an act of the imagination, whereas *Twelfth Night*, by contrast, is saying that what the individual achieves in the way of a meaningful life is a function of what he is and of the values choices he makes. Likewise, both *The Taming of the Shrew* and *As You Like It* show substantial use of wit, as does *Much Ado About Nothing*, but the latter, as we have seen, is distinctly different from the former two. What determines a comedy's direction toward affirmation unlimited or affirmation limited is, rather, and not surprisingly, the playwright's conception of character and action, which in turn determine both comic point of view and view of reality, or we could as easily say, which in turn are finally that balance between comic point of view and view of reality which is characteristic of really good comedy. Really good comedy, is, in its own way, as organic as really good tragedy.

Chapter Three

The Stature of Petruchio

I have previously suggested that a character of stature is the kind of character in whom we could easily take a serious interest, the kind of character with whose consciousness our own consciousness could easily become continuous. But once a comic dramatist decides upon the use of a character of stature he must do two things. First, he must establish such a character within the frame of a comic point of view. Secondly, he must carefully control the development of the character so that it does not exceed limits which are appropriate to the world which the character inhabits. In the case of a farce such as *The Taming of the Shrew* this means that Petruchio's development must be very carefully controlled, since in terms of stature he is about as much as a farce can take. A farce, by definition, depends a great deal on physicality and is not concerned to involve us in substantial psychological complexity. And yet if a farce is merely physical or is confined to the use of static characters it is bound to be dull. Mere physicality is not enough if a comic point of view and a view of reality are to be shaped into a meaningful whole. A lasting farce carefully balances its necessary physicality with some representation of persistent social species whose destiny is both to go on revealing themselves to us and to suggest meanings substantially beyond their identity as social species or type characters.

Our view of Petruchio's character appropriately divides into five parts. The first is the opening definition of character as he arrives in Padua (I, ii, II, i). The second is his verbal duel with Kate and its aftermath (II, i). The third is a brief transition (III). The fourth is the group of taming scenes with Kate in his country house and the subsequent encounter with Vincentio in which the taming process is brought to its successful conclusion (IV, i, iii, v). The fifth is the concluding scene of the play.

The Petruchio we first meet is an engaging balance of farcicality and lyricism, with energy the distinct characteristic of both. In fact, Petruchio at once displays an energy conspicuous by its absence in the first scene except in the character of Kate. Shakespeare in this way uses structure to imply their possible union of spirit and also to separate them in spirit from the rest of the characters in the play. The farcicality involves Petruchio and his man Gremio in both blunt verbal and physical play, with an extended series of puns on the word *knock*—knock at the door, knock someone on the head. Such farcicality functions, as it were, as a metaphor of Petruchio's energetic, straightforward character. He is then quick to make explicit statement of his personal goal in life, "Haply to wive and thrive as best I may" (I, ii, 56), with the emphatic condition that his future bride be:

> *One rich enough to be Petruchio's wife,*
> *As wealth is burden of my wooing dance*
> (I, ii, 67–8)

His very conception of wooing, or to woo, a word repeated many times in the play, is lyrical, as lyrical, perhaps, as birds in the animal kingdom suggested by the

phrase "wooing dance," not to mention the human
equivalent in such things as May Day festivities. It is
no wonder that Petruchio reiterates his theme in lines
that are actually singsong:

> *I come to wive it wealthily in Padua;*
> *If wealthily, then happily in Padua.*
>
> (I, ii, 75–6)

In a tight technical way his alliteration, wealth-wooing,
wive-wealthily, helps to identify his wooing "song" and
requires only a little push to become a delicate but deliberate comic alliteration, such as his later reply to
Gremio's similarly alliterative question whether he "will
woo this wild-cat":

> *Think you a little din can daunt mine ears?*
>
> (I, ii, 200)

or his assurance to Baptista that to win Kate's love is
nothing:

> *for I tell you, father, I am as peremptory as*
> *she proud-minded;*   (II, i, 131–32)

As he later says, he will "woo her with some spirit" (II,
i, 170). As a character of stature Petruchio is altogether
conscious of what that spirit is. It is an earthy lyricism.

If we perceive Petruchio as the lyrical energy of earth
or more specifically as the male urge to sing and woo, we
must note that hyperbolic irony is his hallmark and also,
of course, one of Shakespeare's main devices in the play.
It is a fit device for Shakespeare to use, in that it matches

or fitly projects Petruchio's expansively energetic personality. The obvious joke in process is that once Petruchio knows that Kate is wealthy then he, as a suitor eager for her dowry, must affirm her to be the opposite of what everyone insists that she is. Thus to her father Baptista:

> *I am a gentleman of Verona, sir,*
> *That hearing of her beauty and her wit,*
> *Her affability and bashful modesty,*
> *Her wondrous qualities and mild behavior*
> *Am bold to show myself a forward guest*
>
> (II, i, 47–51)

Or this hyperbolic contrast following the din-daunt alliteration:

> *Have I not in my time heard lions roar?*
> *Have I not heard the sea puff'd up with winds*
> *Rage like an angry boar chafed with sweat?*
> *Have I not heard great ordnance in the field,*
> *And heaven's artillery thunder in the skies?*
> *Have I not in a pitched battle heard*
> *Loud 'larums, neighing steeds, and trumpets'*
>   *clang?*
> *And do you tell me of a woman's tongue?*
> *That gives not half so great a blow to hear*
> *As will a chestnut in a farmer's fire?*
>
> (I, ii, 201–10)

This is a passage worthy of Pope, but Petruchio is only momentarily a mock-heroic character—or we could say that the mock-heroic is another dimension of his versatile character. He asserts in more everyday terms, "I am rough and woo not like a babe" (II, i, 138), but despite the bluntness of his assertion he is sensitively aware that marriage is a question of relationship. His metaphor of marital compatibility is this sensitive hyperbole:

> *And where two raging fires meet together*
> *They do consume the thing that feeds their*
> *fury:*
> . . .
> *So I to her and so she yields to me;*
> (II, i, 133–34, 137)

In sum, he tries to see life for what it is by seeing it as an exaggeration of what it is, or, he sees how close the exaggeration comes in a real (that is, metaphoric) sense to being the reality. It is thus no surprise that his lyrical energy expresses itself as earthy sexual promise: "For I will board her" (I, i, 95), or in the mildly subtle pun, "I know her father, though I know not her" (II, i, 101). But he is also capable of sexual innuendo, as in this reference to Kate as he presents the disguised Hortensio to Baptista:

> *To instruct her fully in those sciences,*
> *Whereof I know she is not ignorant.*
> (II, i, 57–8)

We can be sure that those sciences are sexual in Petruchio's mind, and it is easy to imagine an actor not only making the sexual implication of "those sciences" clear but indeed of hamming it with too distinct a nod or leer in the direction of the audience.

As in the opening definition of Petruchio's character his exaggeration emerges as a metaphor of real feeling, an important signal of that feeling's reality is that he is excited by *proof* of what Kate is. Thus when Hortensio enters with his head broke (by Kate, of course) Petruchio exclaims:

> *Now, by the world, it is a lusty wench;*
> *I love her ten times more than e'er I did:*
> *O, how I long to have some chat with her!*
>
> (II, i, 161–63)

His hyperbolic irony is here distinctly ambiguous and tells us that Kate is literally the kind of woman he wants, a woman with an energy and spirit to match his own. He is acutely conscious of the fact that the woman he marries must be "a lusty wench," or else life, he knows, would be sure to be boring. Metaphorically "a lusty wench" means a happy marriage. Hortensio's early description of Kate as a woman of dowry has a similar metaphoric impact (of which Hortensio is utterly unaware): "And yet I'll promise thee she shall be rich / And very rich" (I, ii, 62–3). When we come to the second phase of the development of Petruchio's character, his first meeting and verbal duel with Kate, we feel it in such a metaphoric sense although the context remains, of course, the joke that Petruchio, motivated by gain, chooses to assert that Kate is the opposite of what she seems to be, or, to put it another way, chooses to assert that what she is, the breaker of Hortensio's head, is in fact greatly to be valued by a man seeking a wife. The shrew, the little mammal with the long pointed nose, or the nagging woman, assumes a true identity only in relative terms, and such a "reversal" is a values comment typical of comedy.

The opening definition of Petruchio's character prepares us to experience his first meeting with Kate as a verbal "wooing dance," a boldly sexual love rehearsal in the kingdom of the imagination which is the farcical now of two people reaching an understanding. After some banter about tails, for example, Kate says farewell, to which Petruchio replies, "What, with my tongue in your tail? nay, come again, / Good Kate; I am a gentleman" (II, i, 218–19). Petruchio, as if imagining them married, offers mock astonishment that she would thus interrupt the love play of the sex act. "Come again" surely refers to a sexual climax, and it is implied that Kate's capacity for sexual enjoyment is what makes her "good." Petruchio is in effect defining a "gentleman" not by the false social norm as one who avoids what some might regard as gross physical play but rather as one who is offended if his physical play is interrupted. Petruchio's essential theme is that of sexual satisfaction and is continued in explicit punning on "cock" in the sense of male sexual organ:

> Katherine: *What is your crest? a coxcomb?*
> Petruchio: *A combless cock, so Kate will be my hen.*
> Katherine: *No cock of mine; you crow too like a craven.*
> Petruchio: *Nay, come, Kate, come; you must not look so sour.* (II, i, 226–29)

Kate is insisting that her lover be truly manly. Petruchio, in response, is assuring her that he is and that she will

come to a sexual climax if she wants to, but he is also, I
think, presenting himself as a lover with the quality of
tenderness. "Nay, come, Kate, come" implies and promises his concern for her sexual satisfaction as well as his
own. Toward the end of their exchange his hyperbolic
irony is clearly a mask—neatly anticipated by his response to Hortensio's broken head—for what as suitor
he really wants to say:

> *I find you passing gentle.*
> *'Twas told me you were rough and coy and*
> *   sullen,*
> *And now I find report a very liar;*
> *For thou art pleasant, gamesome, passing*
> *   courteous*   (II, i, 244–47)

Petruchio is convinced that he and Kate are sexually
compatible and of course compatible in general. His
declaration of love, still with a mask of hyperbolic irony,
is quite straightforward:

> *For, by this light, whereby I see thy beauty,*
> *Thy beauty, that doth make me like thee well,*
> *Thou must be married to no man but me;*
>   (II, i, 275–77)

And also with the mask of hyperbolic irony he becomes
her defender asserting to Baptista:

> *Father, 'tis thus: yourself and all the world,*
> *That talk'd of her, have talk'd amiss of her.*
>   (II, i, 292–93)

His decision is then unequivocal. "Be patient, gentlemen; I choose her for myself" (II, i, 292), and this is followed by perhaps the most meaningful values comment in the play: "If she and I be pleased, what's that to you?" This, it seems to me, asserts the beauty and mystery of personal freedom.

The first two parts of the development of Petruchio's character bring us up to the end of Act II, by which time Petruchio is established as a figure of lyrical energy, boldness, individuality, wit, sensitivity, tenderness, and imagination, a man thoroughly conscious of his individual identity, thoroughly aware of his own values, and able to revel in his awareness of being alive. Such is a character of stature, and Shakespeare faced the problem of what to do with him, how to control his development so that he would remain within a comic point of view, particularly the point of view we call farce. Shakespeare's solution to the problem is first to reassert Petruchio's identity as a creature of farce through Biondello's extended description of his outlandish appearance on the day of the wedding, a description which begins:

> *Why, Petruchio is coming in a new hat and an*
> *old jerkin, a pair of old breeches thrice turned,*
> *a pair of boots that have been candle-cases,*
> *one buckled, another laced, an old rusty sword*
> *ta'en out of the town-armoury, with a broken*
> *hilt, and chapeless;*   (III, ii, 43–7)

And for reinforcement the technique is repeated in Gremio's description of Petruchio's outlandish behavior at the wedding itself (III, ii, 160ff). But when Petruchio enters in his outlandish dress right after Biondello's description, he is not only the creature of farce reasserted but also a man of new assertion. His hyperbolic irony continues but his use of comic alliteration is, significantly, dropped. His ludicrous appearance becomes, as it were, the symbol of new boldness in his values assertion:

> *ha' done with words:*
> *To me she's married, not unto my clothes.*
>
> (III, ii, 118–19)

When, after the wedding, he pretends that he is rescuing Kate, there is a sense in which he is, despite his parody of heroic behavior:

> *Grumio,*
> *Draw forth thy weapon, we are beset with*
>   *thieves;*
> *Rescue thy mistress, if thou be a man.*
> *Fear not, sweet wench, they shall not touch*
>   *thee, Kate.*   (III, ii, 237–40)

It is, in Gremio's phrase, "a mad marriage" (II, ii, 184), and Tranio speaks the truth beyond what he realizes when he comments, "Of all mad matches never was the like" (III, ii, 244). Petruchio is rescuing his "sweet wench" from the non-madness, the sheer staidness, of Padua, for those in Padua are not free in spirit and therefore not truly free.

The fourth part of our view of Petruchio's character, the group of taming scenes in Act IV, is essentially a "hold" in terms of character development. The scenes are highly deliberate farce, with Petruchio (in the first) kicking his servants and throwing food about the stage as he deprives Kate in order to tame her. But there is a new and significant idea: *to fast.* Petruchio's joke is to starve Kate into submission: "And better 'twere that both of us did fast" (IV, i, 176). He is also trying to communicate with Kate in terms of some act that will join them in spirit: "And, for this night, we'll fast for company" (IV, i, 180). The possible religious import of this is, of course, all but lost in the broad physicality and rapidity of farce, but despite this fact Petruchio does *say* that "all is done in reverend care of her" (IV, i, 207). Moreover, at the end of the scene with the Tailor (IV, iii), which is merely a variation of the food-deprivation scene, Petruchio speaks to Kate in terms of an aphorism that is true to his spirit: "For 'tis the mind that makes the body rich" (IV, iii, 174), which perhaps recalls to mind Hortensio's "she shall be rich / And very rich." We may also note that when Petruchio speaks alliteratively, it is hardly with comic effect:

> *we will hence forthwith,*
> *To feast and sport us at thy father's house.*
> (IV, iii, 184–85)

And it is metaphorically important that IV, v opens with Petruchio saying to Kate, "Come on, i' God's name; once more toward our father's." Petruchio has persistently shown respectful address to Baptista as "father," but the context here, it seems to me, enlarges to at least a suggestion of a marriage as a religious quest. This is also confirmed at the end of the scene as Petruchio speaks with respect to the father-figure Vincentio. The highly farcical taming scenes of Act IV are thus delicately counterpointed with suggestive meaning.

The fifth and last part of our view of Petruchio does not involve character development of any significance. What character development there is in the scene belongs to Kate, who asserts her individuality in "obedience" to her lord Petruchio. Petruchio is content to win his wager and to make bawdy jokes, particularly on "coming" in a sexual sense. His joke is implicit when it is announced that Bianca "is busy and she cannot come," but when it is announced that Hortensio's wife "will not come," Petruchio can hardly contain his amusement:

> *Worse and worse; she will not come! O vile,*
> *Intolerable, not to be endured!* (V, ii, 93–4)

From such a context does he draw the final emphasis of "wench" as his epithet for Kate. We can be sure that he speaks from the sure knowledge of his and Kate's sexual compatibility. In fact, it is not too much to say that by the end of the play they have tamed each other sexually (have not *deprived* each other sexually) and in doing so have found new freedom in their relationship to each other. Petruchio's marvelous refrain, spoken for the last time in the last moment of the play, "Come on, and kiss me, Kate," thus expresses what they are as lovers and as human beings.

What Petruchio and Kate are at the end of the play is, then, substantially beyond their identity as social species or mere type characters. Shakespeare has made us feel—however hard we laugh—the quality of a meaningful relationship between the sexes. Or we could as easily say that the identity of Petruchio and Kate as social species or type characters emerges with fullness, with individuality, with ineffable lyricism, and with substantial symbolic power. We are, in a word, *involved* with them over the course of the play though at the same time we see them from the author's framing point of view, and this is a paradox of comedy at its best.

Chapter Four

Shakespeare's Theory of Comedy, First Statement

Critics are often puzzled by the fact that Shakespeare does not bring Christopher Sly back at the end of *The Taming of the Shrew*, but in the light of the view of comedy which we have been developing it turns out that the "problem" is not really a problem at all. The function of the Induction is to establish a comic frame or comic point of view, which is then reasserted, maintained, over the course of the play. There is no need in terms of what comedy is to bring Christopher Sly back into the action. It would, in fact, be gratuitous to do so, since the play has ended and there is nothing new to frame; the idea that Christopher Sly must reappear if the action of the play is to be truly organic does not apply to the true nature and function of comedy. It would, I think, not be terribly jarring to the play if Christopher Sly were indeed brought back for a brief closing comment, but the answer to the question of whether or not he *should* be brought back seems to me clearly to be no.

The Induction is our clue to Shakespeare's theory of comedy. The crucial idea—or at least a crucial way in which it is expressed—is clearly that of the frame, as the Messenger says to Christopher Sly at the end of the Induction:

> *Therefore they thought it good you hear a*
> *play*
> *And* frame *your mind to mirth and merriment*
>   (ii, 137–38 Italics mine.)

This is tantamount to inviting *us* to frame our minds to
mirth and merriment or to announcing that the point of
view of what follows will be comic. To "frame your
mind" is a conscious act of participating in author point
of view. The Induction is itself, however, an example of
the very kind of thing that will follow, for it frames a
view of Christopher Sly as the butt of a joke. We thus
have a compounding of the idea of frames with the
fact implicit that our consciousness moves or is filtered
from frame to frame and thence to character. Since a
play is a thing made, our consciousness is in effect moving
but steadily continuous with that of the author. The device of frames gives us a sense of manipulation, which implies that someone is doing the manipulating. But it is one
thing to announce a frame or to invite participation in a
joke, another to make the frame work as comic or to
make the joke funny. This raises the question of the
conditions under which a joke will go as a joke. Shakespeare, it seems to me, clearly understood that two conditions were vital for the comic to spring into being.

The first of these conditions is that the thing framed
be worth framing, which involves what I have referred
to as the view of reality developed over the course of
the play, a view given its first statement in the Induction. The emphasis of that view is on the value of the
imagination, Sly's dream become a reality which he
eagerly accepts: "Madam, undress you and come now

to bed" (ii, 119). The possibility of sex, impossible in this case anyway, is, not surprisingly, incidental. What is not incidental is the implication of Sly's joyous acceptance. Sly, like Petruchio, but without ironic self-consciousness, revels in the awareness of being alive (his drunkenness is thus a metaphor of health). As a butt of a joke he is a victim, a prisoner of manipulation by others, but in fact he makes those who play the joke on him his victims because his spirit, his essential good will, transcends all. He is thus truly free and embodies the comic spirit as that spirit is affirmation of life. That Shakespeare was conscious of what he was doing theoretically in this respect is suggested by these lines spoken at the end of the Induction by the Messenger to Christopher Sly regarded as a lord:

> *Your honour's players, hearing your*
> *amendment,*
> *Are come to play a pleasant comedy;*
> *For so your doctors hold it very meet,*
> *Seeing too much sadness hath congeal'd your*
> *blood,*
> *And melancholy is the nurse of frenzy.*
>
> (ii, 131–35)

This is, it seems to me, Shakespeare's statement of the medicinal function of comedy. He is asserting that laughter, or the comic spirit, is vital to mental health. Moreover, "too much sadness" is hardly consistent with comedy, or to put it another way, comedy will, for its purposes, shut out from its consideration the quality (as distinct from the fact) of human suffering. This is like saying that a joke can only be funny if it is a joke. Sadness congeals the blood, comedy makes it flow.

The second condition that is vital if comedy is to spring into being is the use of identifying devices. I refer above to "the device of a frame" which gives us a sense of manipulation. It also has the effect of presenting reality as problematic, since it raises the question of which is more real, the frame or the thing framed. This in turn relates to the whole experience of watching a play as a representation of reality and yet in its way more real than what goes on outside the theatre. But the device of a frame exists in relation to other devices, devices which are perhaps thought of as more typical of comedy: exaggeration, surprise, and reversal. We have already referred to Petruchio's use of hyperbolic irony, which is, it seems to me, the chief identifying device of *The Taming of the Shrew*. The point to emphasize is, of course, not the mere use of such a device but the fact that its use is organic, that is, springs from character in action rather than seeming merely to be tacked on as a way to provoke laughter. Kate's character reversal from shrew to good wife is similarly an identifying device—of plot—that is organic. It is also a surprise, or more accurately, the expected surprise. What Shakespeare clearly understood in his early years as a comic dramatist is, it seems to me, that comedy is a balanced combination of devices and that devices are a persistent announcement of intention. But the exact recipe for a given play is his secret and, I think, always will be.

Chapter Five

Bottom and Paradox Compounded

Bottom is the kind of character whom we normally view with detachment, the kind of character with whose consciousness our own consciousness does not easily become continuous. He is a creature of farce, a clown, and thus suggests to us a view of life as spectacle in the extreme. He is patently not a character of stature with the ironic self-awareness, the conscious wit and humor of a Petruchio. Bottom is, moreover, so ignorant—by definition so incapable of change—that one is hardly tempted even to think of him in terms of character development. Though intrepid he may be, he has all of the appearance of a one-dimensional character type; he is, in Puck's plain term, a "rude mechanical." Whereas Shakespeare was concerned to establish Petruchio within the frame of a comic point of view, Bottom is the kind of character who by his very being invites us at once to assume a comic point of view, or we could say that he is the kind of character who functions to set up the frame of a comic point of view. Whereas the use of a character such as Petruchio in a farce necessitates a careful control of character development so that it does not exceed limits which might jar or even spoil the comic point of view, the use of a character such as Bottom would seem to involve almost the opposite problem, how to get some sense of character development out of a character who won't develop.

Not only can a character such as Bottom scarcely be imagined as spoiling a comic point of view, he is a type who could easily threaten it with monotony. That Shakespeare in one way or another was conscious of this problem seems to me strongly suggested by his solution to it.

What Shakespeare does to provide Bottom with the sheer interestingness of a character of stature such as Petruchio or Rosalind, is, as I have already suggested, to "translate" him into a sublimely good representation of the supreme power of the imagination, dream becoming "most rare vision," the play-within-the-play becoming a transcendent and transcendently funny act of the imagination. To do this is, to say the least, no mean trick even for a playwright of the highest skill. In *A Midsummer Night's Dream* Shakespeare renders dramatically the paradox that the men least likely to show imagination show it in abundance.

But this paradox is a fairly obvious thing and does not, I think, get us to the heart of what comedy is as we experience it in *A Midsummer Night's Dream*. It seems to me that a far more important paradox with its focus on Bottom is operative in the play. This second paradox is that Bottom is a character who is altogether controlled by the author and yet at the same time cannot be controlled by the author. The irrepressible Bottom represents complete freedom of the spirit and there is thus a point at which Shakespeare rather than manipulating or controlling him is contemplating him, so that we as spectators and Shakespeare as author lose ourselves in the delight of such contemplation. We have, then, a third possibility in terms of with whose consciousness our consciousness is continuous as we watch comedy. I have suggested that we are *involved* with Petruchio and Kate over the course of *The Taming of the Shrew* though at the same time we see them from the author's framing point of view. I would now suggest that we become involved with Bottom (and, of course, the other rude mechanicals) though at the same time we see him from the author's framing point of view. But we obviously do not become involved with him as a character who possesses stature because he doesn't. What he possesses, it seems to me, is an equivalent of stature, the stature of staturelessness. This stature of staturelessness is, more specifically, an embodiment of qualities, innocence, lyricism, poetic beauty, universal love, personal freedom as the choice of simpleness and duty. As we view Bottom our consciousness is not continuous merely with that of the author in the sense that character limitation helps to create a comic point of view which we share with the author. Our consciousness is, rather, also continuous with the qualities which Bottom embodies. We thus have a direct line to him rather than being obliged to view him exclusively through the author's framing point of view. *A Midsummer Night's Dream* thus repeats and complicates the paradox operative in *The Taming of the Shrew* that character in comedy is not precluded from engaging our consciousness in a continuous way.

An analytic view of the character of Bottom necessarily involves his five appearances in the play, the planning, in Athens, for the presentation of *Pyramus and Thisbe* at Theseus' wedding (I, ii), the rehearsal in the wood, Puck's enchantment of Bottom with the ass's head, and Titania awakening to enthrallment with him

(III, i), Bottom's awakening from his dream (IV, i), the return of Bottom to his cronies in Athens (IV, ii), and, finally, the presentation of the play-within-the-play (V, i). But we may first provide a context for this discussion by considering the question of why Puck has the last word in the play. Why did Shakespeare not let the play end with the presentation of the play-within-the-play? Christopher Sly was not needed at the end of *The Taming of the Shrew*. Why is Puck vital for a last word in *A Midsummer Night's Dream*? Puck is of course—and unlike Sly—an integral part of the action of the play, but this fact does not in itself explain why he makes the final comment.

The answer to the question is that Puck is the final symbol for the comic point of view and the view of reality which Shakespeare has been developing. Puck refers vaguely to "we shadows," but we know that Shakespeare means all actors and more largely all who create an imaginative reality (the playwright included, perhaps, as the ultimate "shadow" because so elusive, so impossible to identify in any kind of specific form other than the play itself). Puck refers to "these visions" and we know, I think, that a glimpse of timeless reality is implied, that art in its ultimate sense implies total order and harmony, or God. He understates his case, "this weak and idle theme, / No more yielding but a dream," (434–35), a dream which is at once everything, insofar as our consciousness of life is everything we have, and nothing, for we always sense our own finitude while longing, consciously or unconsciously, for infinitude. It is, however, most significant that he concludes, "Give me your hands, if we be friends, / And Robin shall restore amends" (444–45). "Give me your hands" is, of course, a conventional request for applause, but it surely refers also to joining hands as an act of brotherly love. Hence the endpoint of the total imaginative act that is the play is a joining of hands to say that we are human and that we are one. It is as if Shakespeare is defining a play (hence life) as his way—his only fit way—of offering his hand. The writing of a comedy thus becomes, not surprisingly, an act of fellowship, the comedy itself an invitation to and an experience of fellowship, and the spectator's applause fellowship's appropriate sound, its symbol.

All of this has a great deal to do with Bottom and the rude mechanicals, for they are preeminently a fellowship. When we first meet them (I, iii) the first line we hear is that spoken by Quince: "Is all our company here?" In context this refers clearly to a theatrical company, but the six characters before us are also a human fellowship in a much larger sense. It is, paradoxically, both important and unimportant that they are formally identified as Quince busies himself casting *Pyramus and Thisbe*. I take Quince, incidentally, to be a pun on *quince*, the pear-shaped fruit whose seeds (of comedy?) are used in medicine and the arts and *quoin*, a cornerstone or, more generally, a wedge-shaped block put to various uses, and also on *coin*, money as signifying value. It is important that they are individuals because fellowship requires the beauty of individual identity. It is unimportant because they exist in the collective identity of "rude mechanicals" or "hempen homespuns." The question that Shakespeare is positing in this scene is whether or not they can put on a play. If they can, we can be sure that only their fellowship, their good will, their good intent, and their ignorance make it possible for them to do so. They are such innocents, and we wonder if innocence will triumph, and if so what the terms of the triumph will be. As a group they embody human fellowship reaching for the power of poetic illusion. I think that we empathize directly with that act of reaching; thus, no matter how detached our view of them may be, it is also spontaneously direct. Their love is, as it were, superior to us and hence they do not need stature.

What we feel as we view the fellowship of the rude mechanicals is, I think, delight, which is to say that we share an aspect or an emphasis of the comic spirit. It delights us to see ignoramuses reaching for art, and there is perhaps a wry implication that Shakespeare as author is presenting a necessary qualification for that act of reaching. But the scene is also funny as farce is funny, and so the question becomes, what does Shakespeare do to unite the kind of laughter we associate with farce and a kind of delight that gives farce a depth with which it is not usually associated. The answer, I think, is that he chooses the right unifying symbol. It is also, in an unsurprising coincidence, a chief identifying device whereby comedy springs into being. This unifying symbol, this identifying device, is the language of the rude mechanicals. Bottom's first words in the play are in reply to Quince's call to the company, "You were best to call them generally," but he means "severally." The play, Quince tells us, is "The most lamentable comedy" of *Pyramus and Thisbe*, and there is, of course, a sense in which when they are the actors the comedy will indeed be lamentable, especially considering the fact that

Bottom must ask if Pyramus is a lover or a tyrant. When Bottom breaks into a sample of verse to display his humour for a tyrant, the verse is appropriately terrible, but Bottom's satisfied comment is, "This was lofty!" (41). Lofty verse is pseudo-eloquent. The rude mechanicals, however, speak as what they are. In speaking as what they are, they are free. In being free and in speaking as what they are, they are eloquent, for, as every semanticist knows, it is the user of language who creates the art of language.

The eloquence of the malapropism becomes a symbol of freedom attained. Perfectly summarizing such eloquence is Bottom's memorable comment toward the end of the scene: "We will meet; and there we may rehearse most obscenely and courageously" (110–11). But it is also significant that he says "adieu" to his companions. He seems to know what it means but he also makes it mean, it seems to me, fellowship. Quince, in the next to the last line of the scene, says, "At the duke's oak we meet" (113). The "duke's oak" thus becomes a symbol of their fellowship, but the difficulty of pronouncing a phrase like "duke's oak" touches the symbol, appropriately, with the absurd. Shakespeare thus exercises perfect control in holding us to a point of view in which we may enjoy the spectacle of inept language, except that his control is so perfect that it is no longer control but rather his rude mechanicals expressing their freedom from all points of view except their own, which in turn is a paradox that Shakespeare intends to express in *A Midsummer Night's Dream.*

In our second encounter with the rude mechanicals (III, i) the delight we feel in their fellowship becomes

the delight of imaginative romping, with the laughter of
farce continuing but perhaps somewhat muted because
the issue at stake is in itself so intriguing. Quince immediately offers a perfect matter-of-fact statement about
the nature of the human imagination. He simply says that
we assert it:

> Bottom: *Are we all met?*
> Quince: *Pat, pat; and here's a marvelous con-*
> *venient place for our rehearsal. This green plot*
> *shall be our stage, this hawthorn-brake our*
> *tiring-house; and we will do it in action as we*
> *will do it before the duke.* (1–5)

Bully Bottom at once asserts that there are things in this
comedy "that will never please" (11). His mistake that
the ladies in the audience might have a literal fear of
swords and killing is the stuff of farce, but behind this
mistake is a right awareness, that poetic illusion must
please. When Starveling is convinced of literal danger
and suggests leaving the killing out, Bottom has the perfect response: "Not a whit: I have a device to make all
well. Write me a prologue" (17–18). His insight that the
confident playwright always has a device to make all well
is perfect in its understanding of the nature of art and
the nature of the human imagination. But his application
of his insight is, of course, faulty. Although he perceives
a prologue as a device of the imagination, he applies the
device literally rather than exploring its imaginative possibilities. This "joke" is compounded arithmetically by
Snout, who calls for yet another prologue to tell that
Bottom is not a lion. Bottom, undaunted, persists in his

confusion of literal event and imaginative reality. He in effect would have a play work both ways; thus on the matter of having a wall through a chink in which the lovers may speak:

> *Some man or other must present Wall: and let him have some plaster, or some loam, or some rough-cast about him, to signify wall; and let him hold his fingers thus, and through that cranny shall Pyramus and Thisby whisper.*
>
> (69–73)

Bottom (following Quince, who would have an actor represent Moonshine) is insightful in suggesting some plaster, loam, or rough-cast to signify the imaginative reality that the actor will project. But Bottom carries his device to the point of absurdity in having the actor hold his fingers up so that Pyramus and Thisbe may speak through them. What Bottom is doing is to press his device of imaginative representation toward a gratuitous literal reality. If a wall is there, it is no problem for us to imagine a chink in it if we see the lovers speaking through it—after all, we are in our senses and know that the stage is a stage and that imagination asserts itself from there. Bottom is persistent in his mistake of offering his audience assurance: the fingers raised as chink assure the audience that the wall is a wall just as the prologue assures the ladies that there is nothing to fear. The true playwright, by contrast, assumes imaginative participation on the part of the audience, imaginative participation that would be contradicted by assurances. Bottom, in other words, has a beautifully right insight but lacks proportion, lacks the talent to apply his insight. He is a weaver who cannot shape his intent to the final pattern which is art. And yet Wall, holding his fingers up to represent a chink, is superbly imaginative as comedy— as lamentable comedy. It is as if Shakespeare creates Bottom the weaver, but Bottom the weaver outdoes Shakespeare, another weaver, of sorts. Shakespeare knows the answers to what makes art, but he also knows that having the answers is not enough to insure that art will be made. Shakespeare knows that no matter how great the artist he, like Bottom, relies finally on intuition, which is brother to humility.

As the rehearsal begins Puck enters and exits with Bottom, who returns with an ass's head. The rude mechanicals disperse in flight, but Snout re-enters to exclaim, "O Bottom, thou art changed!" (117) and Quince, "Bless thee, Bottom! bless thee! thou art translated" (121–22). Clearly the question to be asked is what Bottom's transformation means in terms of the nature of poetic illusion or of imaginative reality. Titania awakens and we witness the working out of Oberon's joke on her, Puck having laid on her eyes the pansy juice that "Will make or man or woman madly dote, / Upon the next live creature that it sees" (II, i, 171–72), that creature naturally being Bottom with the ass's head. The Bottom-Titania scene is farce, the pure spirit Titania falling in love with the gross mortal, the monster, Bottom. Bottom is reminiscent of Christopher Sly accepting his identity as a lord, but the difference between Bottom and Christopher Sly is most important to our understanding of Shakespeare's comic intent. Christopher Sly yields quickly, easily, and naturally to sexual desire. Bottom does not respond

sexually to Titania at all. This is, I think, our clue to the
meaning of his transformation in terms of the nature of
imaginative reality. If Bottom were to possess Titania
sexually, that would surely be a metaphor suggesting that
he possesses immortal love, which in turn would be a
realization of imaginative reality in some ultimate sense.

Instead Bottom wears the ass's head, which surely does
not represent a triumph of imaginative reality, Puck's or
anybody else's. Nor is Titania, victim of Oberon's joke,
suggestive of imaginative reality in triumph, although
her poetic utterance is superb. What triumphs, rather,
is the quality of Bottom's response. His courtesy, mixed
with fear and wonder, is immortal love, whereas Titania
is only nominally immortal love. It is no accident that
Shakespeare has Titania say, "Be kind and courteous to
this gentleman" (167) and at the end of the same speech,
"Nod to him, elves, and do him courtesies" (177). Consider Bottom's response to Titania's declaration of love
"On the first view":

> *Methinks, mistress, you should have little rea-*
> *son for that: and yet, to say the truth, reason*
> *and love keep little company together now-a-*
> *days; the more the pity that some honest*
> *neighbours will not make them friends. Nay, I*
> *can gleek upon occasion.*   (145–50)

This is courtesy. Or consider Bottom's response to the
fairy Peaseblossom:

> *I pray you, commend me to Mistress Squash,*
> *your mother, and to Master Peascod, your*

father. Good Master Peaseblossom, I shall
desire you of more acquaintance too. [To
Mustardseed] *Your name, I beseech you, sir.*
(190–93)

Like Christopher Sly, Bottom is fully cooperating with
the joke being played upon him, but his cooperation
emphasizes his courtesy and ignorant wonder rather than
desire. The ass and the fairy queen do possess each other,
not sexually, but in the beauty of their communication.
It is as if Shakespeare is suggesting that communication
(fellowship) is an ultimate imaginative act. The dream
mood is here, farce all the way, and yet a sublime reality.
The victims of the joke are, paradoxically, not victims
at all. Although we view the scene as farce, our consciousness is continuous also with a beautiful mood, with
the imaginative triumph that is relationship.

From this triumph of relationship Bottom awakens
(IV, i) and delivers his beautiful "I have had a most
rare vision" speech. It is, as I have already suggested, a
moment of, a perception of something beyond one's own
finitude, a mystical assurance, perhaps, that man does
indeed have being. But the nature of that being has been
dramatically defined in the Bottom-Titania scene. There
is, however, an additional thematic wrinkle and new
source of comic delight. Does his dream, "past the wit
of man to say what dream it was," refer to a sexual
ecstasy? Titania has, after all, said "lead him to my
bower" and has referred to every little flower "Lament-
ing some enforced chastity" (III, i, 202, 205). I think
that Bottom is indeed referring to a sexual ecstasy and
that this is part of the comic purport of "man is but an

ass, if he go about to expound this dream." But I do not think that Bottom has possessed Titania in a literal sexual way. I think, rather, that part of Shakespeare's joke on and about sex is that Bottom's vision, his awareness of an ecstatic experience, refers to the immortal aspect of the mortal act. He and Titania communicate, mortal and spirit, and possess each other in that sufficient way, in that sufficient emblem of all that sex could mean. In this way Shakespeare is, I think, wryly saying that sex is finally a kind of dream. Bottom, satisfied lover, awakes.

That Shakespeare intends some wry emphasis on Bottom as lover is confirmed in the following scene (IV, ii), in which the rude mechanicals desperately await him:

> Flute: *If he come not, then the play is marred:*
> *it goes not forward, doth it?*
> Quince: *It is not possible: you have not a man*
> *in all Athens able to discharge Pyramus but he.*
> Flute: *No, he hath simply the best wit of any*
> *handicraft man in Athens.*
> Quince: *Yea, and the best person too: and he is*
> *a very paramour for a sweet voice.*
> Flute: *You must say 'paragon:' a paramour is,*
> *God bless us, a thing of naught.* (5–14)

Bottom is indeed not a paramour, for, one way or the other, there has been nothing illicit in his relationship to Titania. "Paragon" better describes his sweet voice of courtesy, his essential innocence, his stance of wonder. He is a hero to his fellows, which is preposterous, and yet not. But their joy upon his return—though the scene remains farce—could scarcely be called preposterous.

It is, rather, fellowship's moment of ecstasy—"O most courageous day! O most happy hour!" (27–8). And that fellowship, tendering simpleness and duty, now directs itself to a creative act. Bottom is confident, "and I do not doubt but to hear them say, it is a sweet comedy" (43–4). Bottom's final speech in this scene is an ecstasy of anticipation, which he appropriately concludes with, "No more words: away! go, away!" (44–5).

The play-within-the-play climaxes the paradox that characterizes *A Midsummer Night's Dream*. The rude mechanicals put on a play with complete ineptness as their distinguishing characteristic, and yet that ineptness is paradoxically perfect communication. Their mistakes are hilariously perfect in their imperfection. As a result our consciousness is continuous with the quality of the rude mechanicals' perfection though at the same time we see them at the distance at which we normally view ineptness. Shakespeare thus blends complete farcicality with, to put it plainly, the mystery of love, for the play-within-the-play in saying nothing (which is what a bad play says) is also saying that we are human, that we are one. The play-within-the-play is a triumph of fellowship. By the end of *A Midsummer Night's Dream* the laughter of farce is indistinguishable from an ecstatic assertion of being.

The "set-up" for the presentation of the play-within-the-play is easy to describe. The members of the court view the rude mechanicals and we view them both; in fact, the comments by the members of the court are so frequent as to suggest that they are unwittingly participating in a play with the rude mechanicals, that larger play being the play which we view. Although the members of the court provide a perspective on the play-within-the-play, that perspective is bascially not one which we share. Demetrius, for example, makes a joke that is both crude and lame as a joke:

> Theseus: *I wonder if the lion be to speak.*
> Demetrius: *No wonder, my lord: one lion may, when many asses do.* (153–55)

Demetrius shows lack of courtesy, lack of tolerance. Theseus, on the other hand, mollifies Hippolyta's impatience with Moonshine with the comment, "but yet, in courtesy, in all reason, we must stay the time" (258–59). But there is a difference between Theseus' courtesy and his understanding of what is before him. He cannot reach it, he cannot participate in the act of the imagination, despite the fact that he knows what is at stake:

> Hippolyta: *This is the silliest stuff that ever I heard.*
> Theseus: *The best in this kind are but shadows; and the worst are no worse, if imagination amend them.* (212–14)

Shakespeare himself surely believed that the best plays are but shadows (and as shadows challenge the shadowy events we normally call reality). But he surely did not believe that a spectator's imagination could turn a bad play into a good one. What I mean to suggest is that his view of Theseus is wry. He has a sympathetic tolerance for Theseus but regards the speakers of partial

truths as funny. Hippolyta makes this sharp rejoinder
to Theseus: "It must be your imagination then, and not
theirs" (215–16). The first thing that is funny is her
irritable impatience. And yet, it seems to me, she perceives—or at least is saying—that a spectator's imagination cannot turn a bad play into a good play. On the
other hand, she clearly fails to perceive the performance
of *Pyramus and Thisbe* as the true imaginative act that
it is. Such *differences* in the way people think and perceive are to Shakespeare, and to us, funny, but not the
kind of funny that involves uproarious laughter—funny,
rather, in a tickling sense. Perhaps what tickles us is just
the sheer need for tolerance. The set-up for the play-
within-the-play involves, then, the complication of idea
ricochet. The stiff formula of the set-up, sophisticates
watching and commenting upon rude mechanicals, is
enlivened by the dynamics of their involvement, whether
they know it or not, which in turn prompts the dynamics
of our own involvement—whether we know it or not.

What then is to be said of the play-within-the-play as
the rude mechanicals actually perform it? Of central
importance is the theme of communication, which finds
its metaphor, as I see it, in gratuitous assurance that ends
as integral and therefore not gratuitous at all. This exchange, for example, between Theseus and Bottom:

> Theseus: *The wall, methinks, being sensible,*
> *should curse again.*
> Bottom: *No, in truth, sir, he should not. 'De-*
> *ceiving me' is Thisby's cue: she is to enter now,*
> *and I am to spy her through the wall. You shall*

see, it will fall pat as I told you. Yonder she
comes.   (183–88)

Bottom's mistake of assurance seems to me clearly to be
an assertion of care for how others feel, with his care
also a manifestation of his personal freedom, since he
does after all instruct Theseus as to what dramatic art
is all about. Moon's gratuitous assurance to the court
beautifully asserts, much as Quince does in III, i, the
human imagination as a fact:

> *All that I have to say, is, to tell you that the*
> *lanthorn is the moon; I, the man in the moon;*
> *this thorn-bush, my thorn-bush; and this dog,*
> *my dog.*   (261–63)

It is as if Moon, without knowing it, is challenging the
spectators, both the members of the court and us, to participate in the act of the imagination and to affirm it as
a fact. The decent and courteous Theseus speaks beyond
his own intent when he shortly says, "No epilogue, I
pray you; for your play needs no excuse" (361–62).
Shakespeare is telling us that imagination does not have
to be justified, it simply is.

It is Theseus who gives us what is probably the best
metaphor to explain the comic success of the performance of *Pyramus and Thisbe*, his response to Quince's
prologue: "His speech was like a tangled chain; nothing
impaired, but all disordered" (124–25). This disorder is,
of course, paradoxically a form of order, imaginative
order. Quince opens his prologue with, "If we offend, it
is with our good will" (108), and we know that good

will transcends and transforms ineptness. Were this not
the case the members of the court might be insulted by
what from another mouth might be a savagely witty
conclusion to a prologue: "The actors are at hand and
by their show / You shall know all that you are like to
know" (116–17). The rollicking bawdy is another aspect of the tangled chain, as in Thisbe's address to Wall:

> *My cherry lips have often kiss'd thy stones.*
>
> (192)

It would, I think, hardly be going too far to suggest that
here is the theme of lovemaking as an aspect of intent,
of love's own innocence and good will, not to mention—
for society's sophisticates—love's own sense of humor
that recalls to us Petruchio and Kate. The linguistic disorder of the play-within-the-play is fundamentally
parody, bad verse made even worse and thus best for
comic purposes, as, for example, Pyramus' address to
night:

> *O grim-look'd night! O night with hue so*
> *   black!*
> *O night, which ever art when day is not!*
> *O night, O night! alack, alack, alack,*
> *I fear my Thisby's promise is forgot!*
>
> (171–74)

And yet the same Pyramus, the same Bottom, turns to
Wall when he holds up his fingers to represent a chink
and says, "Thanks, courteous wall," (179) and the tangled chain is suddenly not tangled at all, not even disordered.

So at the end of *A Midsummer Night's Dream* the rude mechanicals have triumphed. It has been a sweet comedy. Accepting that imagination is knowledge, we know all that we are like to know. We have met at Ninny's tomb, have listened to the moon, which shines with a good grace. We see a voice, and reality has been but a slumbering, a shadow. As we share the caring of the rude mechanicals, we are free, and as Bergson has said, "All that is serious in life comes from our freedom."

Chapter Six

Shakespeare's Theory of Comedy, Second Statement

I have suggested that the Induction to *The Taming of the Shrew* is our clue to Shakespeare's theory of comedy, with the crucial idea clearly that of the frame—"And frame your mind to mirth and merriment." This is, of course, what I have spoken of more broadly as the necessity for the comic playwright to establish a comic point of view. What is important relative to theory of comedy as we examine *A Midsummer Night's Dream* is not merely the repetition of the idea of a comic point of view or of a comic frame but rather the variant form which that idea takes. As we move from *The Taming of the Shrew* to *A Midsummer Night's Dream* we move from the idea of framing our minds to mirth and merriment to the idea of slumber, of dream, "dream away the time" (I, i, 8). To frame our minds to mirth and merriment is to act deliberately, to know, or at least to assume we know, what reality is. To slumber, to dream, is to let ourselves move into a world in which reality is problematic, a world which the poet's pen turns to elusive shapes. A comedy as an organization of ideas thus becomes a much more open form, a much more complex form. In terms of a theory of comedy what *A Midsummer Night's Dream* implies is the paradox that framing our minds to mirth and merriment or but slumbering here is also imaginative surrender. For comedy the crucial question is whether or not that surrender can be total. Shakespeare's answer, I think, was yes, and so he wrote *A Midsummer Night's Dream*. It is his only comedy—and I believe the only comedy in the world—in which there is total imaginative surrender, that is, in which our consciousness quickly becomes totally continuous with the thing itself as opposed to continuous with an author point of view as well as the thing itself. It is as if Shakespeare is saying—in anticipation of Samuel Johnson's Preface—that there can at least be one time in which the spectators are not always in their senses and do not know from the first act to the last that the stage is only a stage and that the players are only players. That time is when imagination becomes the supreme reality, when the spectators are enthralled, when poetic illusion is no longer illusion but all the reality there is. Those who cannot experience it are, as it were, cast into outer darkness, but not in the sense of missing out on the intellectual or intellectually oriented perception, for the knowledge of truth at stake in our perception of *A Midsummer Night's Dream* is, ultimately, a function of love—"And I do love thee" (II, i, 159)—rather than of brains.

What I mean to suggest is that *A Midsummer Night's Dream* is a paragon of a comedy and of comedy generally. Whereas *The Taming of the Shrew* is, roughly speaking, duplicatable, *A Midsummer Night's Dream* is unduplicatable. In this context its similarities as comedy to *The Taming of the Shrew* become all the more fascinating and also allow us better to appreciate the differences. Both plays make use of spectacle in the extreme. In *The Taming of the Shrew* the spectacle is the taming process, with Petruchio as a clown of stature clowning his way through it. In *A Midsummer Night's Dream* the spectacle focuses on the rude mechanicals, Bottom chiefly, and culminates in the play-within-the-play. In both plays there is strong emphasis on individuality transcending type, Petruchio and Kate coming alive as individuals in *The Taming of the Shrew* and Bottom being "translated" in *A Midsummer Night's Dream*. A related idea which the plays have in common is the freedom of the spirit implied by individuality. Both plays end with what amounts to an assertion of being, an imaginative order, an awareness that imagination is truth and knowledge. Both make use of language as an identifying device, as, in fact, a kind of spectacle in and of itself, Petruchio's hyperbolic irony in *The Taming of the Shrew* and the eloquence of the malapropism, of linguistic ineptness, in *A Midsummer Night's Dream*. Both are distinguished by lyricism, which may be regarded as the essence of many things, the comic spirit as a spirit of affirmation, a sense of delight and laughter, a quality related to the mystery of love, to the soul of love, whether between the sexes or more general, poetic illusion as a fact of our experience, as a purging of mortal grossness, revelling, joyousness, health, charm, delight, balance, the discourse of wonders, the announcement of intention that is so vital if comedy is to spring into being, and the end result, as Oberon expresses it, "and all things shall be peace" (III, ii, 377).

What Shakespeare as a writer of comedy obviously understood was that comedy's devices, or characteristics, *must* repeat themselves and yet at the same time always be subordinate to the individuality which is the new organic whole. This is, of course, another way of saying that he clearly understood that a comic point of view must be established and maintained and that a view of reality must be developed over the course of the comedy, but his intricate mind goes on from there to play with what we might call "all of the rules" in terms of paradox, and thus to establish the very act of his own playing as a rule itself, each bit of play involving play with it, and so on ad infinitum. It is in some such sense that *A Midsummer Night's Dream* is a play that discusses art and the art of comedy while it itself is the thing that it discusses. This is, in my view, not the kind of thing that can be done twice.

Chapter Seven

Rosalind and Incremental Development of Character in Comedy

As You Like It is Rosalind's play and Rosalind is a character of stature, a character with whose consciousness our own consciousness may easily be continuous. As I have previously suggested, she is so interesting that she could if she developed from a very strong beginning become so strong, so deeply engaging our consciousness continuously with hers, that she could move the whole point of view of the play outward to the shaded area of serious drama; for this reason Shakespeare develops her character gradually—at least gradually for comedy— and she does not assume full stature until the full development of her relationship with Orlando in the middle and later part of the play. The question remains, however, how as a character of stature she relates to the purposes of comedy, what limits as necessary for comedy are placed on the development of her character. I have also previously suggested that the comic spirit of *A Midsummer Night's Dream*, its deep beauty apart from laughter, is akin to the comic spirit of *As You Like It*, and that imaginative love in *As You Like It* is a perception of something beyond one's own finitude. *As You Like It* thus connects with "most rare vision" as we find it in *A Midsummer Night's Dream*. And yet *A Midsummer*

Night's Dream, whatever else it is, is an enormously funny play and *As You Like It* is not. So our question tends to compound: how as a character of stature does Rosalind relate to the purposes of comedy when those purposes are not directed in a preeminent way toward the end of laughter? How does Shakespeare keep *As You Like It* from becoming a dull or a fatuous affirmation of the comic spirit? The answer in general is, of course, the stature, the sheer interestingness of Rosalind, but we must now take a close look at this as process.

Rosalind appears in ten scenes in *As You Like It,* her first two appearances (I, ii and I, iii) being those in which she is not in disguise. Since her not being in disguise is clearly a unit of her character development and since she is only offstage for a few minutes between I, ii and I, iii, we may examine both scenes at once. The scenes, moreover, tie together in other ways. For example, in her very first speech in the play Rosalind refers to "a banished father" as her reason for not being merry, but then some three hundred fifty lines later, in I, iii, Duke Frederick banishes her so that she is shortly on her way in disguise to the forest of Arden. We are prompted to ask how the tyranny of two banishments suits the purposes of comedy. Of course exposition in the first scene of the play makes clear that Rosalind's father, Duke Senior, is living in the forest "like the old Robin Hood of England" in something of a "golden world" (I, i, 121–25) and so vengeance and suffering are shut out from comedy as we expect them to be. But the question remains, how does Shakespeare tell us that what we have before us is indeed comedy? One is prompted at once to argue that if Duke Senior is, as things go, happy in Arden then his banishment is paradoxically liberty, and this is like a placard placed on the stage and reading "comedy." Then, as is typical of comedy, things are made explicit and we find Celia saying at the very end of Act I, seconds before we move to the forest of Arden itself, "Now we go in content / To liberty and not to banishment" (iii, 139–40). But the question has, I think, a more persuasive and a different kind of answer.

This more persuasive answer has to do with the structure of Act I. What Shakespeare in effect does is to set up Rosalind in terms of her relationship to a whole series of other people. The first of these, and antecedent to the action of the play, is her relationship to her father. The second is her relationship to Celia, which is the first time we meet them both. The third is her relationship to Touchstone, who breaks in on the Rosalind-Celia dialogue, the fourth is her relationship to Orlando, who comes to try the wrestler Charles with "the strength of my youth" (I, ii, 181), and the fifth is her relationship with Duke Frederick, who has usurped his brother's kingdom and banished him and will now banish his niece. These relationships in turn classify into two main groups, one of which is the relationship of Rosalind to Orlando. It is a simple case of romantic love. Rosalind makes a succession of comments indicating clearly to us that she is gone on Orlando; for example, "The little strength that I have, I would it were with you" (I, ii, 207–08). And Orlando sounds like Romeo in his response to Rosalind: "But heavenly Rosalind!" (I, ii, 301). We thus confront two forms of liberty, liberty in banishment and liberty in romantic love and hence the play declares its intention to be comedy. We are not surprised that Orlando throws the wrestler Charles nor that Rosalind ad-

mits her love to Orlando: "you have wrestled well and
overthrown / More than your enemies" (I, ii, 266–67),
nor that Rosalind, when Celia suggests that she hem the
burs in her heart away, reiterates the point: "I would
try, if I could cry 'hem' and have him" (I, iii, 20).

The second group of relationships with Rosalind
serves to balance or to counterpoint the instantaneous
but potentially boring fires of love at first sight. Before
Celia and Rosalind enter for the first time, the wrestler
Charles makes the comment to Oliver, "and never two
ladies loved as they do" (I, i, 116–17). An innocent
enough remark, perhaps. But toward the end of Act I we
find Celia saying to Rosalind, "Rosalind lacks then the
love / Which teacheth thee that thou and I am one"
(I, iii, 98–9). We may at least wonder—as perhaps
Charles has wondered—if Celia's sexuality is normal.
Celia reasons, moreover, that if her uncle had banished
her father, "so thou hadst been still with me, I could have
taught my love to take thy father for mine" (I, ii, 11–12).
And her comment on courtship is essentially the axiom,
flirt, but don't go too far: "but love no man in good
earnest; nor no further in sport neither than with safety
of a pure blush thou mayst in honour come off again"
(I, ii, 29–31). To which Rosalind, with what I take to
be wryness, replies, "What shall be our sport, then?"
Rosalind seems to perceive that love involves risk and
that the reward is well worth the risk. Celia, by contrast,
perceives little that would define her as mature. Touchstone enters and engages in this enigmatic banter with
Rosalind:

Touchstone: *No, by mine honour, but I was
bid to come for you.*

Rosalind: *Where learned you that oath, fool?*
Touchstone: *Of a certain knight that swore by
his honour they were good pancakes and
swore by his honour the mustard was naught:
now I'll stand to it, the pancakes were naught
and the mustard was good, and yet was not the
knight forsworn.*   (I, ii, 63–71)

"That oath" ostensibly refers to "by mine honour,"
which in turn suggests that Touchstone, because of Rosalind's sensitivity to it, or perhaps to its intonation, is
mimicking Rosalind's father. But there is, I think, another level of meaning here. "I was bid to come for you"
is a vulgar remark, an oath of vulgar wit—and without
the hilarity of farce we have seen at the end of *The Taming of the Shrew.* The knight swearing by his honour
is a fatuous knight, one who substitutes words for the
test of reality, and thus one scarcely fit to hold onto
power, to his kingdom. Rosalind's response is a perempt
dismissal of Touchstone. What the Rosalind-Celia, Rosa-
lind-Touchstone relationships suggest, then, is Rosalind's
individuality and maturity, her readiness to deal with life.
This is the woman who in a few moments will be falling
head over heels in love with Orlando, and this is also the
woman who will say to Duke Frederick when he banishes her, "Yet your mistrust cannot make me a traitor"
(I, iii, 58), to which Duke Frederick replies, "Thou art
thy father's daughter" (I, iii, 60). Although Duke Frederick clearly shows jealousy of Rosalind for her superi-
ority to Celia—"she robs thee of thy name" (I, iii, 82)—
perhaps he is banishing Rosalind because in some twisted
way he blames her for Celia's immaturity or even her
leaning toward sexual abnormality—"we still have slept

together" (I, iii, 75), says Celia to her father, who may wince to hear it. All of this, it seems to me, makes Rosalind's simple case of romantic love not so simple at all. Rosalind has an awareness of the world around her against which she is obliged to measure—and is capable of measuring—romantic love and its possibilities.

By the end of Act I, then, we have a strong sense of Rosalind as a heroine of comedy in the sense of a heroine of stature who will persistently and dynamically, that is, in dynamic relationship to the world around her, affirm. But what does Shakespeare then do with his heroine in terms of writing a comedy? There are, I think, two basic answers to this question. The first is the motif of disguise. Helen Gardner puts the matter most aptly: "The trial and error by which we come to knowledge of ourselves and of our world is symbolized by the disguisings which are a recurrent element in all comedy, but are particularly common in Shakespeare's." The second basic answer is clearly concomitant to the first, namely, that Rosalind will experience her trial and error in a particular place, the forest of Arden, which with its spectacle of pastoral conventions is a fit locale for comedy and which draws our minds away, as it were, from certain complexities which it is not fit for Shakespeare to pursue in comedy. Moreover, Shakespeare not only provides and develops a fit locale for comedy, he also puts appropriate restraint on the development of Rosalind. She appears in disguise as Ganymede for the first time in I, iv, a short scene which functions to emphasize the depth and honesty of her emotion—"I could find in my heart to disgrace my man's apparel and to cry like a woman" (4–5)—and her mature attitude toward love in contrast to the silly conventionality of the shepherd Silvius. We do not see Rosalind again until III, ii, which is to say that she has been offstage for almost four hundred lines. By the time we do see her we are, I think, conditioned to accept her experience as the delightful process of discovery. Shakespeare thus manages to keep character dynamic but functioning to the purposes of comedy. This is quite a different thing from the "hold" which he put on the development of the character of Petruchio.

The development of Rosalind's character in III, ii must be seen, then, in terms of the scene's development as comedy. Orlando enters and is absurd as a romantic lover hanging his verses on a tree: "Hang there, my verse, in witness of my love" (1). Corin and Touchstone enter and discuss country and city life, Corin's definition of the true laborer suggesting an ideal for any society and yet making the speaker seem absurdly self-congratulating and pretending something beyond the reality that men, even in the forest of Arden, can attain: "I earn that I eat, get that I wear, owe no man hate, envy no man's happiness, glad of other men's good, content with my harm, and the greatest of my pride is to see my ewes graze and my lambs suck" (75–9). Rosalind enters reading Orlando's verses, though Shakespeare makes her wait over one hundred lines before Celia identifies her lover specifically. Orlando's verses tell us, as it were, that Arden, whatever else it is, is a place for poetry. But Touchstone at once parodies the verses and as a clown of vulgar jest concludes his parody:

> *He that sweetest rose will find*
> *Must find love's prick and Rosalind.*

(117–18)

Rosalind's response is one of resigned exasperation: "Peace, you dull fool! I found them on a tree" (121). Surely there is a suggestion here that this is a tree of knowledge, but the context of absurd romantic love holds the suggestion to the purposes of comedy. If disguise symbolizes the trial and error by which Rosalind will come to self-knowledge, it surely symbolizes also a shutting out of whatever in the past does not help her as an individual toward what she most needs; thus what is carried over from Act I is Rosalind's longing for a love relationship that, shall we say, is liberty rather than a banishment to the sterility of love conventions or to the sterile vulgarities of the world's Touchstones, however much charm or wit such vulgarities may have on the surface. The emphasis of III, ii is, in other words, on the liberty of courtship, with courtship in turn one of the comic spirit's readiest instruments of affirmation.

Rosalind herself uses the word: "an old religious uncle of mine taught me to speak, who was in his youth an inland man; one that knew *courtship* too well, for there he fell in love" (361–64, my italics). She is speaking to Orlando. When he enters after Celia has properly identified him as the writer of the verses, Rosalind makes her sudden choice: "I will speak to him like a saucy lackey and under that habit play the knave with him" (313–14). Thus begins what Harold Goddard has pointed to as the love rehearsal in the kingdom of the imagination, which is, of course, much the same as what Helen Gardner refers to as trial and error leading to self-knowledge. Courtship is, after all, a thing of the imagination or it is nothing, and it is, moreover, the imagination engaged in a process of trial and error. Furthermore, what we now have in *As You Like It* is a double disguise, Rosalind as Ganymede as Rosalind. This compounding process is, it seems to me, an important part of the delight of comedy. In fact, in III, ii *As You Like It* becomes amusing. We may recall Rosalind's comment to Celia early in Act I, "What shall be our sport, then?" The answer is here—the sport is courtship.

What Shakespeare has done in moving from the Rosalind of Act I to the Rosalind of III, ii has been to deepen the engagement of our consciousness with Rosalind and the whole concept of a search for imaginative love, for values, which she embodies. We could say, that is, that he has transformed what we first identify as romantic love into the infinitely more beautiful and individual thing we call imaginative love. He takes the absurdity of courtship, or rather courtship as a thing of absurd process, and vivifies for us the fact that courtship's absurdity as process is vital to its success as communication between two human beings. Orlando is merely absurd when he says, "Hang there, my verse, in witness of my love," but he is both absurd and beautifully, individually, engaging when he says to Rosalind, "I am he that is so love-shaked; I pray you, tell me your remedy" (384). His assertion is a proclamation of individual identity. Rosalind answers it in kind: "There is none of my uncle's marks upon you: he taught me how to know a man in love; in which cage of rushes I am sure you are not prisoner" (385–87). Rosalind's technique is simple; she is telling Orlando that he is not in love in order to elicit from him convincing evidence (communication) that he is. But if we look more deeply, we find that what she is really *asking* Orlando is whether or not his love is deeply spiritual.

She casually referred to her uncle in the cliché term "an old religious man," but surely we must grant a literal meaning to this as present in the depths of her psyche. Moreover, when she says "he taught me how to know a man in love" she surely—and perhaps wryly—means "know" not only in the sense of recognize but also in the sense of the deepest of all relations between man and woman; she is promising Orlando the ultimate in sexual and spiritual contentment. This is amusing because it is oblique, in, as it were, the raiment of disguise to suggest a trial and error probe. This disguise soon becomes double disguise as Rosalind will search further for love's meaning, Orlando to imagine Ganymede as "his love and mistress" (428). Rosalind as Ganymede as Rosalind will pretend to "cure" Orlando of his love, that is, she will test their compatibility, their real understanding, the certainty of their knowledge—carved on the tree of personality's inner depths—that they are in love. Orlando agrees to the test—"With all my heart, good youth" (454). Rosalind responds with beauty's own simplicity, with courtship at its wry best, "Nay, you must call me Rosalind" (455).

The next time we see Rosalind (III, iv) she is reacting to the fact that Orlando has failed to show up for their love rehearsal—"why did he swear he would come this morning, and he comes not?" (21). She says, "I will weep" (1) but we are scarcely prepared to believe this. In fact, she has the appearance of a conventional lady in a conventional situation. What Shakespeare is doing is simply to continue *As You Like It* with the stuff of comedy, which is also emphasized by Phebe's rejection of Silvius, a situation to which we see Rosalind react in III, v. This does not, however, mean that the development of Rosalind's character is to be abandoned. It means, rather, that her character development will at this point be oblique in contrast to the directness, or oblique directness, of her exchange with Orlando in III, ii. To put the matter another way, Shakespeare takes utterly conventional material—Rosalind moaning that Orlando has not shown up for what to her is their date and Phebe rejecting Silvius—and counterpoints it with Rosalind as a character of stature. It is as if Shakespeare is choosing what is most boring in order to expose what is most interesting, in this case the character of Rosalind. Thus the content of her banter with Celia becomes very important; for example, the marriage ideal implied by her description of Orlando: "his kissing is as full of sanctity as the touch of holy bread" (III, 14–15); or concern for whether or not there is "truth in him" (III, 22) or "verity in love" (III, 25). Similarly the content of the dialogue centered on the Phebe-Silvius relationship serves to define Rosalind's inner self; for example, her search for what Phebe with mere conventional rhetoric describes as "So holy and so perfect is my love" (III, v, 99), or Rosalind's advice to Phebe as a description of Rosalind herself: "down on your knees, / And thank heaven, fasting, for a good man's love" (III, v, 57–8), which recalls the fasting motif in *The Taming of the Shrew*, Rosalind to communicate with Orlando in terms of an act that will join them in spirit.

What makes the dull convention of Rosalind as an impatient lover (albeit in disguise) interesting in fact is that her conventional impatience implies a deep loneliness and a longing and a struggle with both. At the opening of IV, i her rejection of Jaques—"I fear you

have sold your own lands to see other men's (22–3)—
becomes in this context an affirmation of her own deter-
mination to find an answer to her loneliness and to find
it, of course, in love. The rejection of Jaques is also a
fit preface to her next meeting with Orlando. There is
even, I would say, the desperation of loneliness in her
beautifully simple and matter-of-fact assertion to Orlando, "And I am your Rosalind" (64), an assertion
which also represents disguise working as a trial and error
process leading to self-knowledge. Thus Rosalind's impatient lyric appeal, "Come, woo me, woo me" (68)
makes us want to experience the wooing process because
we sense that self-discovery will be involved. The wooing process is, in other words, dynamic, and not just a
question of a repetition of the act of love rehearsal in
the kingdom of the imagination. It is with great lyric
intensity that Rosalind defines for Orlando what the
marriage pattern will be like, and her definition is also a
discovery of what she herself is in the context of the disguise and wooing game:

> Rosalind: *Now tell me how long you would
> have her after you have possessed her.*
> Orlando: *For ever and a day.*
> Rosalind: *Say 'a day,' without the 'ever.' No,
> no, Orlando; men are April when they woo,
> December when they wed: maids are May
> when they are maids, but the sky changes
> when they are wives. I will be more jealous of
> thee than a Barbary cock-pigeon over his hen,
> more clamorous than a parrot against rain,
> more new-fangled than an ape, more giddy in*

*my desires than a monkey: I will weep for
nothing, like Diana in the fountain, and I will
do that when you are disposed to be merry; I
will laugh like a hyen, and that when thou art
inclined to sleep.* (143–56)

The scene ends with Rosalind asserting to Celia in lyric
wonder, "O coz, coz, coz, my pretty little coz, that thou
didst know how many fathom deep I am in love!"
(209–10). We can, I think, fairly assume that Rosalind's
loneliness has been as deep as she discovers her love to
be, and the image of depth seems perfect in terms of
what Shakespeare is attempting with regard to character
development.

The development of the character of Rosalind, how
deep she is in love, is climaxed in IV, i. What remains
is the resolution of that character development. Shakespeare's essential technique from IV, iii to the end of the
play is if anything to intensify the disparity between
utterly conventional material and the interestingness of
Rosalind. In IV, iii she encounters Orlando's brother
Oliver, who recounts the story of his "conversion" to a
life of virtue after being rescued from a lioness by Orlando. Since we have not seen Oliver since the first scene
of Act I, this has all the appearance of exceedingly
mechanical plot manipulation. But in the same scene
Rosalind, addressing Silvius, has given this statement, in
the negative, of her marriage ideal in response to Phebe's
message: "What, to make thee an instrument and play
false strains upon thee! not to be endured!" (67–9). We
can be sure that Rosalind's marriage will be a relationship
of exchange—a true fellowship—rather than a relation-

ship of mutual exploitation. When Oliver relates Orlando's apology to Ganymede and reveals "this napkin / Dyed in his blood" (155–56), Rosalind swoons. It is a swoon of conventionality, of course, but it also suggests what Oliver then calls it, "a passion of earnest" (171–72). It *can* suggest this because we know that Rosalind's commitment in love to Orlando is a commitment of her total self, her being. The larger context, however, is that the joke is now on Rosalind, who has been so busy playing her joke on Orlando. It is amusing that Rosalind insists that her swoon was "counterfeit," and the word echoes like a refrain, compounding the amusement, our delight in her embarrassment.

The resolution of Rosalind's character development completes itself in V, ii and V, iv. Oliver and Celia are paired—"no sooner looked but they loved" (V, ii, 36–7) —and Rosalind, who has "conversed with a magician, most profound in his art" (V, ii, 65–6), gets ready to abandon her disguise. She is doubtless tickled with her triumph when she reiterates the idea to Orlando: "I say I am a magician" (V, ii, 78), and tickled with her own lyric promise to Orlando of deep sexual and spiritual contentment: "I will satisfy you, if ever I satisfied man, and you shall be married to-morrow" (V, ii, 123–24). Tomorrow comes and Rosalind enters with Hymen, the god of marriage. Rosalind presents herself as a gift to Orlando: "To you I give myself, for I am yours" (V, iv, 123), and Hymen prompts the group to "a wedlock-hymn" (V, iv, 143). What makes the entrance of Hymen appropriate at the end of the play?, we are prompted to ask. The thematic appropriateness to celebrate a group of marriages is obvious, but there is, I believe, a deeper reason. Rosalind has already sufficiently defined the spirit of a true marriage. The extremity of convention—the sudden entrance of the god of marriage —thus returns us to where we ought to be, with the essential character of Rosalind, "human as she is" (IV, ii, 75).

The development of Rosalind's character is incremental in a manner appropriate to the purposes of comedy. The broad pattern of that development is from romantic love to imaginative love to loneliness and longing to the wooing process as self-discovery and to the lyric wonder of love and finally to love as a passion of earnest, a commitment of being with the self offered as a gift. But there is not, as we would expect in serious drama, a curve of self-discovery that involves us in an ever deepening intensity, and thus Rosalind's loneliness and longing, for example, is not treated as a dramatic rendering of personal crisis, as a scene in which the quality of loneliness is preeminently at stake. But we must be careful not to assume serious drama as a norm, for *As You Like It* does involve us in a deepening emotional way. Shakespeare could hardly convince us emotionally in Act I of the wooing process as self-discovery and of the lyric wonder of love. Much of the delight we feel in response to *As You Like It* is, in other words, a function of our involvement with the character of Rosalind as she uses courtship, or mock courtship, as a means to better understand herself and her own values. Similarly, Shakespeare could hardly bring on Hymen in Act I and some would make a case that to bring him on in Act V is not effective dramaturgy, even for comedy, which might well be true were it not for the Rosalind-

Hyman identity as the true spirit of marriage. Our emotional involvement is, in sum, distinctly with Rosalind at the end of the play, but it is an emotional involvement that involves the paradox that our consciousness may be continuous both with the consciousness of the author—viewing life as spectacle—and with the consciousness of his heroine. In this connection it is interesting to ask what seems to have become the classic question for *As You Like It.* Why does everyone return to court at the end of the play? Is not the forest of Arden happiness enough? Is loving Arden and leaving for court in fact a contradiction? The answer to this, it seems to me, is simple enough. The best locale for the process of self-discovery is not the best locale for the working out of the results of that process. What lovers need after an Arden of wooing or of instant love is a chance to prove —to live—the meaning of it all under conditions of challenge. In the case of Rosalind we must remember that she has implied a discreet sense of mortality in her comment that the sky changes when maids are wives. Her move back to court is an acceptance of mortality but a hungry desire to make it affirm immortality.

Chapter Eight

Shakespeare's Theory of Comedy, Third Statement

As we move from *The Taming of the Shrew* and *A Midsummer Night's Dream* to *As You Like It* we move from the ideas of framing our minds to mirth and merriment and of slumber or dream to the idea of courtship as imagination engaged in a process of trial and error, or of self-discovery. We have, of course, seen courtship as imagination in *The Taming of the Shrew*, but trial and error, or self-discovery, is new. Although Bottom's "most rare vision" is in the spirit of self-discovery, it is by definition not the thing itself because Bottom is essentially not capable of a discovery of himself. What *As You Like It* adds to Shakespeare's theory of comedy is depth characterization as process. Although Petruchio also exemplifies depth characterization, Shakespeare could exploit that depth by displaying it as process only if he chose to write a different kind of play. *The Taming of the Shrew* commits itself to the taming process rather than to depth characterization as process.

I have suggested that *A Midsummer Night's Dream* expresses the paradox that the life of the imagination is more real than any literal reality. Bottom is "translated" into something one would not ordinarily expect him to be. In the structure of *As You Like It* there is a significant parallel to this. In *As You Like It* Shakespeare takes the utterly conventional—to my mind in the sense of the most boring—and "translates" it into life at its most interesting, that is, into the utterly real. It is a playful thing to do, a thing fit for comedy. What makes it possible for him to succeed in a task so difficult is Rosalind, for she "translates" *As You Like It* from a thing of conventionality or even of utter dullness into its opposite. In this way Shakespeare makes depth characterization wholly functional to the thing he is saying. *As You Like It* coheres so well as a play because Rosalind is in a constant interaction with a relatively dull world, or worlds. Shakespeare uses the extremity of convention as a foil for Rosalind, and Rosalind as a foil for the extremity of convention.

Rosalind's relation to the extremity of convention is a structural device rather than what I have referred to as a chief identifying device of comedy. *As You Like It* has such a chief identifying device but unlike the hyperbolic irony of *The Taming of the Shrew* or the malapropisms of *A Midsummer Night's Dream* it is not linguistic—although one could easily emphasize Rosalind's lyricism as such a device. The chief identifying device of comedy in *As You Like It* is, I would say, the device of disguise, which I take to be equivalent to the idea of a play-within-a-play. Disguise in *As You Like It* thus recalls the Induction to *The Taming of the Shrew* and the presentation of the lamentable comedy of *Pyramus and Thisbe* in *A Midsummer Night's Dream*. One of its chief functions is, of course, to insist upon the comic point of view, the playwright's view of life as spectacle, or we could recall that Helen Gardner refers to disguise as "a recurrent element in all comedy." But in *As You Like It* Shakespeare transforms disguise into a symbol of imaginative love and of the values quest which imaginative love implies, that is, into a symbol of the sport of courtship. Shakespeare's theoretical understanding of comedy thus once again emphasizes the necessity of unifying a device and meaning, which is tantamount to saying that in *As You Like It* he selects a perfect means to realize a coincidence of comic point of view and a view of reality.

Whereas the Induction to *The Taming of the Shrew* and all of *A Midsummer Night's Dream* show what amounts to explicit author concern with theory or with the nature of the art form which he is creating, *As You Like It* is relatively unconcerned with such matters. By its nature, however, comedy is itself its own subject and we are particularly aware of this fact as the play concludes. The last scene of *As You Like It* defines the comic spirit. Hymen sings of universal peace and concord, of the human fellowship:

> *Then is there mirth in heaven,*
> *When earthly things made even*
> *Atone together.*   (V, iv, 113–15)

Wedlock is celebrated, "a wedlock-hymn we sing" (143). The activity appropriate to such a celebration is, of course, song and dance; thus Duke Senior:

> *Play, music! And you, brides and bridegrooms*
> *all,*
> *With measure heap'd in joy, to the measures*
> *fall.*   (184–85)

And he defines the end of comedy in the last lines of the play:

Proceed, proceed: we will begin these rites,
As we do trust they'll end, in true delights.

(203–04)

The melancholy Jaques, echoing the comment made at
the end of the Induction to *The Taming of the Shrew*,
is the unwitting spokesman for the medicinal function
of comedy:

> *give me leave*
> *To speak my mind, and I will through and*
> *through*
> *Cleanse the foul body of the infected world,*
> *If they will patiently receive my medicine.*

(II, vii, 58–61)

Orlando becomes a spokesman for individuality in the
manner of Petruchio—"If she and I be pleased, what's
that to you?" (II, i, 307)—when he responds to Jaques'
comment on Rosalind, "I do not like her name" with
"There was no thought of pleasing you when she was
christened" (III, ii, 282–84). Following his conversion,
Oliver comments, "From miserable slumber I awaked"
(IV, iii, 133), recalling, faintly, Bottom's awakening
speech, or even Demetrius' "Why, then, we are awake"
(V, i, 202). To be awake is to live with heightened
sensitivity and to affirm the beauty and wonder of life
and the mystery of personal freedom. What Bottom perceives in a vision, Rosalind realizes in an act. The other
characters in comedy share the vision, share the comic
spirit, but to a degree appropriate to what each one is,
and thus with Demetrius and Orlando Shakespeare is
gently and wryly ironic. The comic spirit is poetry, for,

as Touchstone says, "the truest poetry is the most feigning; and lovers are given to poetry, and what they swear
in poetry may be said as lovers they do feign" (III, iii,
19–22). What Shakespeare means by "the most feigning" is, I think, the most perfect in imaginative conception and, wryly, the most daring in how that feigning
is carried out. He was, I think, persistently amused at
himself.

Chapter Nine

Beatrice, Benedick, Dogberry and the Perfection of Freedom

I have previously suggested that the plays under discussion divide into two groups, with *The Taming of the Shrew*, *A Midsummer Night's Dream*, and *As You Like It* representing the playwright's choice to move toward affirmation that is virtually unlimited (as an act of faith is virtually unlimited) and *Much Ado About Nothing* and *Twelfth Night* representing his choice to move toward affirmation that is clearly a thing of limits (as the life we know constantly is). As we turn from *As You Like It* to *Much Ado About Nothing* we turn, then, from a love rehearsal in the kingdom of the imagination to "a merry war" between Beatrice and Benedick. The merry war is a love rehearsal, is the sport of courtship, but the crucial difference between the two plays as comedy is that in the characters of Beatrice and Benedick the social order is internalized by intellect and they themselves are unable to sing beyond intellect, whereas Rosalind, for all of her intelligence, is a spontaneous singer and also in her spirit free of an oppressive social order. The question arises, in *Much Ado About Nothing* is the mystical assurance that man does indeed have being gone and in its stead do we have an existential affirmation? Or, if the love of Beatrice and Benedick is not rare vision, then what is it? But, as I have indicated, we can hardly look at Beatrice and Benedick apart from Dogberry because

Dogberry connects to them in spirit, takes over the play, as it were, and expands the emphasis they give to individuality. So our purpose in this chapter will be first to offer a descriptive definition of the love of Beatrice and Benedick as "a merry war" and then to relate Dogberry to it.

The opening of *Much Ado About Nothing* is most significant in terms of establishing a context for what is to follow, for the group at Messina is waiting for Claudio and Benedick to return from war. To Beatrice war is absurd, and she wastes no time in objecting to Benedick wasting his time in its absurdity: "I pray you, how many hath he killed and eaten in these wars?" (I, i, 42–3), and, "He hath every month a new sworn brother" (I, i, 72–3), that is, she disdains the practice of swearing brotherhood and sees no meaning in being a brother in arms because war to her is futility. As she makes her objection to war, Leonato describes her relationship to Benedick in terms of a war metaphor, "a kind of merry war" (I, i, 63) between them and "they never meet but there's a skirmish of wit between them" (I, i, 63–4). The Messenger describes Claudio as doing "in the figure of a lamb, the feats of a lion" (I, i, 14–15), which I would take to imply that Claudio is physically slight but furious in battle, which in turn might suggest war as a means for men to rid themselves of their aggressions and "prove" their manhood, the very kind of thing that Benedick disdains as futile and resists as part of an oppressive social order. The opening of the play involves, in other words, a significant values contrast between the rational and the irrational, between human behavior that is meaningful and human behavior that is ridiculous waste.

What we mainly *experience* as the play opens is, however, the wit of Beatrice and her first skirmish of wit with Benedick. Their exchange is strongly a comedy of insult; for example:

> Beatrice: *I wonder that you will still be talking, Signior Benedick: nobody marks you.*
> Benedick: *What, my dear Lady Disdain, are you yet living?*
> Beatrice: *Is it possible disdain should die while she hath such meet food to feed it as Signior Benedick? Courtesy itself must convert to disdain, if you come in her presence.*
>
> (I, i, 117–24)

The function of such wit is essentially twofold. It is first—and quite obviously—a simple method for lovers to communicate; we know that the more they seem to be against each other the more they are destined for each other's arms. As a corollary to this, they are placing themselves apart from the group, as indeed their values will insist they do anyway. The second function of their wit is as a release for genuine aggressiveness. The implication is that if Beatrice could not rail against war, she would surely go mad. Similarly, if Beatrice and Benedick could not rail against each other, they would be without a way to release their inner tensions. This is, of course, part of the sport of courtship wherever it is found, but trenchant wit, or insult, gives the sport a particular character. It is, I think, not going too far to suggest that Beatrice and Benedick are in the figures of lambs —creatures of civilization—but they have the inner emotions of lions, that is, they have emotions, tensions, that must find release, must be sublimated. For them to find release in the game of oblique courtship is surely a healthy thing, whereas to have "killed and eaten in these wars," to have killed and enjoyed it, is surely a sick way for civilized men to find release for their pent-up energies.

A health-sickness contrast is continued for the rest of the opening scene, but the subject of war is dropped and in its place we find the subject of courtship and marriage. Benedick and Claudio, alone on the stage, discuss Leonato's daughter Hero. Although Benedick describes himself as "a professed tyrant to their sex" (I, i, 169–70), it is clear that he is actually an honest and sensitive man. In apparent jest he says, "and being no other but as she is, I do not like her" (I, i, 176), but we are made to wonder *why* he does not like her. Claudio insists that he is not joking, and Benedick responds with a question that is witty but trenchant: "Would you buy her, that you inquire after her?" (I, i, 181). Claudio's response is conventional love rhetoric: "Can the world buy such a jewel?" (I, i, 182), and a worldly-wise Benedick replies, "Yea, and a case to put it into" (I, i, 183). The values contrast is simple. Benedick has a healthy outlook toward life, Claudio a sick one. For Claudio a human being may be a commodity. Benedick knows that conventional lovers who "sigh away Sundays" (I, i, 203) are false in heart. In this connection it is significant that Don Pedro says to Claudio "*if* you love her" (I, i, 223, my italics), and also that Don Pedro says to Benedick, "I shall see thee, ere I die, look pale with love" (I, i, 249–50). Don Pedro knows that Benedick is a man of real feeling, and he does not, significantly, make a similiar comment to

Claudio. When Claudio asks Don Pedro if Leonato has any son, the worldy-wise Don Pedro is quick to respond that Hero is Leonato's only heir. The implication is trenchant; Don Pedro knows that Claudio cannot think of marriage except in terms of money. This trenchancy is, moreover, reiterated in the next scene in Borachio's matter-of-fact identification of Hero as "the daughter and heir of Leonato" (I, ii, 56–7). Claudio's response to Don Pedro is conventional love rhetoric which is hilariously funny as an exposure of his own falseness:

> *But now I am return'd and that war-thoughts*
> *Have left their places vacant, in their rooms*
> *Come thronging soft and delicate desires,*
> *All prompting me how fair young Hero is,*
> *Saying, I liked her ere I went to wars.*
>
> (I, i, 303–07)

Don Pedro then offers to woo Hero for Claudio:

> *I know we shall have revelling to-night:*
> *I will assume thy part in some disguise*
> *And tell fair Hero I am Claudio*   (322–24)

"Revelling to-night" and the disguise motif tell us at once that the values contrast which we have seen will continue to be treated from a comic point of view. Moreover, Don Pedro, in addition to having a sense of values that links him in spirit to Benedick has himself a good sense of humor—he may as well woo for Claudio considering what he perceives to be the real nature of the prospective marriage of Claudio to Hero.

The masks are soon donned (II, i), but not before Beatrice makes a key values statement in favor of individuality, recalling Petruchio's "If she and I be pleased, what's that to you?" and Orlando's "There was no thought of pleasing you when she was christened." Beatrice's ostensible subject is the relation between the generations:

> Antonio: *Well, niece, I trust you will be ruled by your father.*
> Beatrice: *Yes, faith; it is my cousin's duty to make curtsy and say 'Father, as it please you.' But yet for all that, cousin, let him be a handsome fellow, or else make another curtsy and say, 'Father, as it please me.'* (II, i, 53–9)

Beatrice is trenchant but is hardly advocating disobedience unless just authority takes the form of tyranny, of a truly oppressive social order. Her emphasis, rather, is on the utter necessity for the individual to make values choices and values affirmations, an emphasis which is then repeated in her masked exchange with Benedick— they will follow the leaders in every *good* thing. The scene moves quickly to its main purpose, the "set-up" of the joke to be played on Beatrice and Benedick. An identifying element of the set-up is Benedick's hyperbole to the effect that anything is better for him than Beatrice; for example:

> *Will your grace command me any service to the world's end? I will go on the slightest errand now to the Antipodes that you can*

> *devise to send me on; I will fetch you a tooth-*
> *picker now from the furthest inch of Asia,*
> *bring you the length of Prester John's foot,*
> *fetch you a hair off the great Cham's beard, do*
> *you any embassage to the Pigmies, rather than*
> *hold three words' conference with this harpy.*
>
> (II, i, 271–78)

Leonato comments that Beatrice "mocks all her wooers out of suit" (II, i, 364–65), and then Don Pedro, who has successfully wooed in Claudio's stead, decides to spend the week until the marriage of Claudio and Hero undertaking "one of Hercules' labours; which is, to bring Signior Benedick and the Lady Beatrice into a mountain of affection the one with the other" (I, i, 380–82). Although Beatrice and Benedick have in effect invited witty counteraction to their apparent refusal to conform to society's ways, it is likely that Don Pedro wants to balance the rather mechanical marriage of Claudio and Hero with the real thing, the union of Beatrice and Benedick. He does, in any case, do his plotting with the delight of the comic spirit.

Until the idea of gulling Beatrice and Benedick for their own good is born in the mind of Don Pedro, the play is very much a matter of values probing, with trenchant wit held within the frame of the comic point of view but potentially strong enough to move outside that frame. It is thus not surprising that Shakespeare pursues the joke to be played on them with farcical deliberateness—Don Pedro, Claudio, and Leonato speaking so that Benedick will overhear them—in order to hold in check, for the purposes of comedy, the values probing that has been taking place. This is also tantamount to a decision to put a hold on their character development. Such a hold works well in *Much Ado About Nothing* for two basic reasons. The first is that lovers normally think of love, that is, of themselves, and not of the social order and all of its values crises. The second is that Beatrice and Benedick as two intellectuals *ought* to yield to their emotions. Don Pedro perceives this fact, but there is a difference between his perspective and the author's. The difference between the farcical deliberateness of Don Pedro and the farcical deliberateness of Shakespeare lies in the fact that Shakespeare has, as we would expect the author of a comedy to have, a comprehensive sympathy for the intellectual as a creature of desperate need desperately absurd in that need. Values probing followed by farce is Shakespeare's choice of a pattern, and the pattern is his witty way of suggesting that even intellectuals may be free.

The gulling of Benedick is executed in II, iii. That Shakespeare intends a strong focus on the absurdity of the intellectual, on the paragon of animals as utterly ridiculous, is clearly suggested by the use of two soliloquies spoken by Benedick at the beginning and at the end of the gulling. In the first soliloquy Benedick muses on the possibility that he, like Claudio, may "after he hath laughed at such shallow follies in others, become the argument of his own scorn by falling in love" (II, iii, 10–12). "May I be so converted and see with these eyes?" (II, iii, 21–2) Benedick asks. But we must ask why he does not see through Claudio at this point. To say that Shakespeare has put a hold on Benedick's character development would in this instance be mechanical. The reason must lie, rather, in what Benedick is. He does not see through Claudio because he is too generous, too good a friend, to see through him. Except that it might corrupt his spirit, Benedick could use a little of Don John's worldliness and cynicism. Benedick's description of Claudio exposes Claudio to us beyond Benedick's intent:

> *He was wont to speak plain and to the purpose, like an honest man and a soldier; and now is he turned orthography; his words are a very fantastical banquet, just so many strange dishes.* (II, iii, 18–21)

Although Benedick is musing at the possibility of what outward form being in love might take, we know that this is the Claudio of false rhetoric, the Claudio interested in Hero as Leonato's heir. Although Benedick is intelligent and sophisticated he thus becomes, relatively speaking, absurd in his innocence. It is as if when he says "till all graces be in one woman, one woman shall not come in my grace" (II, ii, 30–1) that he does not even know that all graces might be in Beatrice. He is (a little like Hamlet) defeated by his own intellect and is thus absurd. He is also absurd and absurdly flawed in his romantic idealism, for no man may reasonably expect all graces to be in one woman although that is happily what he may find if he lets nature take its course. The second soliloquy, spoken after Benedick has overheard the remarks of those playing the joke on him, compounds the absurdity. His first words, spoken after we have witnessed some one hundred thirty odd lines of farcical deliberateness, are hilariously funny: "This can be no trick" (II, iii, 227). Benedick then proceeds to rationalize his emotion, which is another absurd flaw of the intellectual. But although he is aware that society may ridicule him as one who has railed so long against marriage yielding at last to the emotion, he rejects social pressure as an influence; "quips and sentences" and "paper bullets of the brain" will not awe him from "the career of his humour" (II, iii, 49–51), his love. The real point of the gulling is thus that Benedick despite his utter absurdity is free. The pattern is then repeated for Beatrice (III, i), who falls for the trick as readily as Benedick. At the end of III, i Beatrice is alone on stage and, like Benedick, is absurd, but, I would say, less absurd because more sure of her values and more lyrically intense. As with Christopher Sly and Bottom, there is a point at which the victim is no longer a victim but is free:

> *What fire is in mine ears? Can this be true?*
> *Stand I condemn'd for pride and scorn so*
> *much?*
> *Contempt, farewell! and maiden pride, adieu!*
> *No glory lives behind the back of such.*
> *And, Benedick, love on; I will requite thee,*
> *Taming my wild heart to thy loving hand:*
> *If thou dost love, my kindness shall incite thee*
> *To bind our loves up in a holy band;*
> *For others say thou dost deserve, and I*
> *Believe it better than reportingly.*
>
> (III, i, 107–16)

We are now ready for the entrance of Dogberry because the love of Beatrice and Benedick has been defined. It is not rare vision but it is a beautifully individual affirmation of a thing felt, of existence.

As I have previously suggested, Dogberry connects to Beatrice and Benedick in spirit, for all three are strongly individual, Dogberry beautiful in his innocence and Beatrice and Benedick beautiful in their love. Although Beatrice and Benedick are tricked into confessing their love, they are nevertheless free, and the character of Dogberry is summed up in his marvelous comment, "it is an offence to stay a man against his will" (III, iii, 87–8), that is, man is by nature free. The deliberate farcicality of the gulling of Beatrice and Benedick is continued in the hilarious farce, particularly of malapropism, which we witness in Dogberry and the members of the watch. One of the malapropisms may serve to illustrate a thematic link. Dogberry uses the phrase "desartless man" (III, iii, 9) for "deserving man." And yet "desartless" also suggests "without art," which is surely what Dogberry and his men are. As the sophisticated Beatrice and Benedick are gulled, they become artless lovers, and thus they are united in spirit with Dogberry and his men and, we might add, with Shakespeare as comic dramatist whose attitude toward life is one of universal sympathy and tolerance. A vital qualitative link between Beatrice and Benedick and Dogberry and his men is their lyricism as it becomes a values emphasis. In this connection it is appropriate to lift some phrases from the context of hilarious farce in III, iii and to think of them as related to the characters of Beatrice and Benedick and to their experience of love: "good men and true" (1), "give God thanks" (19), "your honesty" (56), "a man who hath any honesty in him" (68), "the most peacable way" (60–1), "a merciful man" (64), "depart in peace" (73), "to offend no man" (86).

The idea of peace as an implied lyrical refrain is particularly important because it takes us back to the first scene and the return from war. It also leads us to see Claudio in his maltreatment of Hero as a man of war in the sense that he is estranged from his essential being—sin, Paul Tillich reminds us, being "man's estrangement from his essential being." Beatrice and Benedick are, of course, not estranged from their essential being but are, rather, forcefully concerned to express it. But Dogberry, magnificent as universal love, defines them as creatures of existential affirmation rather than of mystical assurance. Dogberry possesses mystical assurance, as Bottom does, but this is precisely why Shakespeare has him stumble to justice and then turn the play back over to the lovers, for Shakespeare in *Much Ado About Nothing* is concerned with the life we know as a thing of limits. There is great philosophical poignance in the word *nothing*, but the comic spirit cloaks it—and triumphs over it—with *much ado*.

When Dogberry takes his leave of Leonato after the villains have been exposed, he says, "God restore you to health!" (V, i, 334). The implication is that the society which Leonato represents is not healthy in Dogberry's sense, which is surely the sense in which he would "write God first" (IV, ii, 21). One might speculate that the idea of original sin is involved. Paul Tillich suggests that the term "original sin" should be reinterpreted as "the stage of estrangement for which, in spite of its tragic character, we are personally responsible and out of which the concrete acts of estrangement from ourselves, from others, and from the meaning of our being, follow." Leonato was responsible for estrangement from his essential being when he leaned toward acceptance of the accusation of dishonor against Hero: "Death is the fairest cover for her shame / That may be wish'd for" (IV, i, 116–17), and "let her die" (IV, i, 156). In this context the Friar's strategem to set things in order is a grace whereby "the load of sorrow" (V, i, 28) is lifted from Leonato. What maintains the latter part of the play, particularly V, i, as comic in spirit, or point of view, is our knowledge that Dogberry has bound the "naughty varlet" (IV, ii, 74) Borachio; thus all is well and we need wait only for a resolution of events. Borachio confesses, and Claudio at once says to Leonato, "Impose me to what penance your invention / Can lay upon my sin" (V, i, 283–84). Leonato's reply is the substitution motif:

> *my brother hath a daughter,*
> *Almost the copy of my child that's dead,*
> *And she alone is heir to both of us:*
> *Give her the right you should have given her*
> > *cousin,*
> *And so dies my revenge.*　　　(V, i, 298–302)

It is a strong irony that Claudio is offered an "heir." He gets what he deserves, an heir rather than the ultimate rewards of the spirit, and yet more than he deserves. It is only moments later that Dogberry is saying, "God restore you to health!" Claudio is the beneficiary of the mercy of the comic spirit, and he will, after all, have to live with what he is. And so will Beatrice and Benedick, who have more to recommend them personally.

The play ends with couples on their way to the chapel. Benedick speaks the last words of the play, "Strike up, pipers" (V, iv, 130). As in *As You Like It* the activity appropriate to nuptial celebration is song and dance, but Benedick is existential matter-of-fact compared to Duke Senior's trust that "these rites" will end "in true delights." Moreover, Benedick's call to the pipers is immediately preceded by his comment on Don John, whom armed men are bringing back to Messina: "I'll devise thee brave punishments for him" (V, iv, 129–30). For a world where the assurance of being is mystical, we must go back to the last words which Dogberry speaks in the play, to Verges, "Come, neighbour" (V, i, 336–37). The perfect beauty and simplicity, not to mention the reverence, of such fellowship is not granted to Beatrice and Benedick. When Benedick says to Beatrice, "Thou and I are too wise to woo peaceably" (V, ii, 75), he is asserting not only the quality of a dynamically joyous relationship, a perfection of freedom, but also that relationship's limitation.

Chapter Ten

Shakespeare's Theory of Comedy, Fourth Statement

Since *The Taming of the Shrew*, *As You Like It*, and *Much Ado About Nothing* all involve courtship as imagination, it is appropriate to ask how the three plays relate to one another in this respect. If to the idea of courtship as imagination *As You Like It* adds the idea of trial and error, or of self-discovery, then to what extent does *Much Ado About Nothing* show trial and error, or self-discovery? But first, a caution. Our generalizations naturally tend to take on a formulaic appearance. Who, after all, is to say—or would want to say—that *The Taming of the Shrew* does not project some sense of courtship as a process of trial and error, or of self-discovery? Who is to say with finality that *Much Ado About Nothing* is either more like *The Taming of the Shrew* with respect to its treatment of courtship or more like *As You Like It*? These matters are relative, and where the balance is struck will inevitably involve a strong subjective response. With this caution I would offer my own judgment that with respect to the treatment of courtship *Much Ado About Nothing* is essentially closer to *The Taming of the Shrew* than to *As You Like It*. I would say that there is more self-discovery involved in the courtship of Beatrice and Benedick than in the courtship of Petruchio and Kate, but I do not see Beatrice and Benedick approaching Rosalind and Orlando in this area. The fundamental reason for this is that Shakespeare does not treat Beatrice and Benedick in terms of depth characterization as process. Beatrice and Benedick have depth, but process is a different thing.

It is thus crucial that Shakespeare puts a hold on their characters as he moves to the farce comedy of the joke played upon them, and it is also crucial that Dogberry enters the play, for if he did not then surely Shakespeare would have to devise either a way to develop Beatrice and Benedick or some continuation of farce that would keep us interested in their courtship as process. If it takes Dogberry to hold the comic point of view in the latter part of the play, particularly with regard to V, i, then without Dogberry Beatrice and Benedick or someone like Don Pedro would have to be responsible for holding the comic point of view in the latter part of the play, which in terms of plot would simply mean be responsible for apprehending the villains. Following *The Taming of the Shrew* and *A Midsummer Night's Dream* what is new in *Much Ado About Nothing* is, then, not trial and error, or self-discovery, added to courtship as imagination, but something else, not easy to define.

That something else might be called courtship as wit. But Petruchio and Kate and Rosalind and Orlando show wit, and so the question becomes what is the essential difference, or what is the emphasis? The answer to this question resides, I think, in wit as trenchancy or a form of values probing. Freud has emphasized that jokes take their origin from the unconscious and are in the service of unconscious purposes or of purposes that are reinforced by the unconscious. He also emphasizes that effective jokes often show great substance or intellectual content. This is a kind of emphasis that applies, it seems to me, with particular cogency to Beatrice and Benedick, especially to Beatrice, as well as to Don Pedro. To put the matter another way, wit makes *Much Ado About Nothing* a psychologically serious play, but since comedy by its nature is psychologically serious—that is, must develop a meaningful view of reality—it must be emphasized that this psychological seriousness is something that we *feel* as we view the play. Our consciousness is continuous with it in a way that is tantamout to our consciousness being continuous with the conciousness of character while at the same time sharing the author point of view. This seriousness is inevitably a seriousness that goes far beyond the fact of wit, or wit as a device of comedy. It is a seriousness that is integral to the total structure of the play.

In fact, as I have indicated, Shakespeare is concerned in the structure of *Much Ado About Nothing* not to let the seriousness of the play get out of hand, not to let it break out of the frame of the comic point of view. His problem was, I think, intensified by the fact that he is dealing with an existential seriousness as opposed, say, to a serious rendering of an essentially religious affirmation. Although comedy does not preclude a world of questions and doubts, of unwholesome values and villainy, it can include them in an important way only if the comic writer is particularly skillful in blending the elements of comedy. *Much Ado About Nothing* shows Shakespeare as a master of such blending.

When Shakespeare came to write *Much Ado About Nothing* he understood that it was necessary to balance the play's existential seriousness with a considerable amount of farce. He also wisely limits the treatment of the villain Don John. Don John is man estranged from his essential being. He acts against Claudio, as men estranged from their essential being act against each other, that is, as men at war with themselves war with each other. He is perhaps "sick in displeasure" (II, ii, 5) to Claudio because as "a plain-dealing villain" (I, iii, 33) he abhors the phoniness of Claudio and is jealous of the phony's success. Both Don John and Claudio are prisoners of themselves, are not free men. But the emphasis of *Much Ado About Nothing* is on their failure—even to the extent of what I take to be Claudio's skin-deep penance. However, that failure is far overshadowed by the success of Beatrice and Benedick. Leonato says of Beatrice that she swears she never will make her affection known to Benedick and "that's her torment" (II, iii, 129–30). Her torment, however, is not an estrangement from her essential being but rather part of the dynamics of her personal freedom. Although she and Benedick inhabit a world in which freedom is a dilemma and something of a tormenting mystery, neither dilemma nor torment block them from expressing what they genuinely are.

Chapter Eleven

Sir Toby and the World
of Anti-Dream

As we move from *Much Ado About Nothing* to *Twelfth Night* we move from a comedy whose affirmation is clearly a thing of limits to a comedy whose affirmation is a thing of greater limits, so much so that *Twelfth Night* may be said to create a world of anti-dream. The world of dream which we have seen in *A Midsummer Night's Dream* emphasized dream in the sense of vision, a moment of, a perception of something beyond one's own finitude, a mystical assurance, perhaps, that man does indeed have being. In *Twelfth Night* what we have instead of Bottom's dream "past the wit of man to say what dream it was" is a world in which neurosis is distinctly present. But the point of view of *Twelfth Night* is, as I have shown, definitely comic. The question of moment is, then, how the dark side of *Twelfth Night*, *Twelfth Night* as a world of anti-dream, relates to and is held within this framing point of view, and this question becomes in turn the question of how Sir Toby is a character suitable to comedy as an art form, how as a character of stature he is held within the play's framing point of view. A corollary question must be the nature of Sir Toby's character development, particulary how it compares to the incremental development of Rosalind's character. But since the events of *Twelfth Night* are of the order of hilarious farce, this question comes to in-

volve a relationship of extremes, with farce as one extreme and character stature as another. The nature of
this relationship will, of course, hardly be a return to
The Taming of the Shrew.

We first meet Sir Toby in I, iii, a scene that is patently
farce with a strong emphasis on witty jesting. The witty
jest is, however, a thing of provocative content. Sir
Toby's first words are in response to Olivia's mourning
for her brother:

> *What a plague means my niece, to take the*
> *death of her brother thus? I am sure care's*
> *an enemy to life.*   (1–3)

What he opposes is her excess, and yet, his wit notwith-
standing, he himself is quickly revealed as a creature of
excess, a man who stays up all night "quaffing and
drinking" (14), and Maria suggests that he confine himself "within the modest limits or order" (9), which
thematically emphasizes, of course, that he lives a life
of disorder. But excess and disorder are part of his character type, are readily acceptable as premises of his character; we must be careful, that is, not to emphasize
seriousness or seriousness of point of view in this scene
unless Shakespeare nudges us in that direction, which is
precisely what he does. The key exchange is mainly between Maria, who has been called a "fair shrew" (50)
by Sir Andrew, and Sir Andrew:

> Maria: *Fare you well, gentlemen.*
> Sir Toby: *An thou let part so, Sir Andrew,*
> *would thou mightst never draw sword again.*

> Sir Andrew: *An you part so, mistress, I would*
> *I might never draw sword again. Fair lady, do*
> *you think you have fools in hand?*
> Maria: *Sir, I have not you by the hand.*
> Sir Andrew: *Marry, but you shall have; and*
> *here's my hand.*
> Maria: *Now, sir, 'thought is free;' I pray you,*
> *bring your hand to the buttery-bar and let it*
> *drink.*
> Sir Andrew: *Wherefore, sweet-heart? what's*
> *your metaphor?*
> Maria: *It's dry, sir.*
> Sir Andrew: *Why, I think so: I am not such*
> *an ass but I can keep my hand dry. But what's*
> *your jest?*
> Maria: *A dry jest, sir.*
> Sir Andrew: *Are you full of them?*
> Maria: *Ay, sir, I have them at my fingers'*
> *ends: marry, now I let go your hand, I am*
> *barren.*   (63–84)

Sir Andrew's question, "what's your metaphor?", is our key to this passage. Metaphor is a mode of communication and the people involved know it as such a mode and enjoy using it, accept it as their life style. What "metaphor" here involves is double or multiple meaning. Sir Toby's "would thou mightst never draw sword again" is an obvious use of sword to mean phallus, a use which could easily be indicated by the actor's inflection and typical of the gay vulgarity of the tavern, the kind of vulgarity that most of us can healthily enjoy. But why, in comedy, does Sir Andrew repeat the first part of Sir Toby's comment, "An you part so, mistress, I would I might never draw sword again"? It is clear that he is gayly accepting Sir Toby's reference to the sword, but his meaning of "part so" is, it seems to me, more than merely "depart." It is, rather, a vulgar reference to Maria parting or spreading her legs for sexual relationship, the reference being vulgar in a negative sense because the concept of sex involved is carnal and disrespectful. When Sir Andrew suggests to Maria that she shall have him by the hand he surely refers to her holding his phallus in her hand. Sir Andrew's consciousness of this meaning is suggested by his quickness in offering his hand for her to shake, hence a witty offering of his phallus for her to shake. Maria's suggestion that he bring his hand to the buttery-bar and let it drink would in this context be an invitation to enjoy sexual relationship with her except that she precedes it with "Now, sir, 'thought is free,' " which seems to suggest that as far as she is concerned his sexual activity can be fantasy. Sir Andrew seems puzzled by her remark when he asks, "Wherefore, sweet-heart?" The puzzlement is, I think, explained later, but also in metaphor.

In II, iii Sir Toby refers to Maria as "a beagle, true-bred, and one that adores me" (195–96), to which Sir Andrew responds, "I was adored once too" (197), meaning that he has had sexual relations with her. No wonder he is puzzled by her metaphor, which Maria calls "dry." Sir Andrew is quick to pick up the word, "I am not such an ass but I can keep my hand dry," which would seem to have two possible meanings, either that he can masturbate without getting his hand wet (perhaps further implying that he is sterile) or that he can stimulate Maria sexually without getting his hand wet, that is, keeping it out of her vagina. But Sir Andrew is still puzzled and asks what her jest in reference to "dry" is. She responds with a pun on dry. "A dry jest, sir," means an emotionless jest, a sarcastic jest rendered in a matter-of-fact way, but also a jest without semen (as a comment on Sir Andrew's sexual prowess and a re-joinder to the idea of keeping his hand dry) and a withered jest, that is, a jest that is a sign of the debility of age. "Dry" in reference to bread also means without butter, which metaphorically suggests that Maria is sexually starved; even in the buttery-bar there will be no sexual satisfaction for her, for the men in her life lack semen (butter for the bread), that is, cannot give her love. When Maria says to Sir Andrew, "now I let go your hand, I am barren," she is confessing to a life of futility. She is dry in the sense of barren. She is aware that her life is barren of meaning. If Freud's emphasis that jokes take their origin from the unconscious and are in the service of unconscious purposes or of purposes that are reinforced by the unconscious applies with cogency to Beatrice and Benedick, it applies with even deeper cogency to Maria, Sir Andrew, and Sir Toby, whose souls are laid bare by their own language games. Shake-speare makes clear that the subject of the above exchange is not—as in *The Taming of the Shrew* with its delight-ful vulgar wit, even that of Bianca—the relationship be-tween the sexes but rather sex without relationship.

At the end of the scene Sir Toby and Sir Andrew banter about the zodiacal sign Taurus. When Sir Toby asks, "were we not born under Taurus?" (146–47), he is surely thinking of the bull as a sexual symbol. Sir Andrew says, "Taurus! That's sides and heart," to which Sir Toby replies, "No, sir; it is legs and thighs" (148–49). In the context of the exchange between Maria and Sir Andrew Sir Toby emerges here as preoccupied with sex, his mind filled with it to excess just as he is filled to excess with drink. He is, moreover, expressing his contempt for Sir Andrew, rather than expressing fellowship to the man who is "drunk nightly" (38) in his company. In general Sir Toby uses Sir Andrew as a commodity of his own sick pleasure, which is to say, he mocks the very idea of fellowship. To mock fellowship is to opt for a world of anti-dream, a world in which the care and concern, the sweet courtesy of the rude mechanicals, is conspicuous by its absence. What Sir Toby *is* is shortly defined in explicit terms by Olivia. The Clown first defines what a drunken man is like.

> *Like a drowned man, a fool and a mad man:*
> *one draught above heat makes him a fool, the*
> *second mads him; and a third drowns him.*
>
> (I, v, 139–41)

Olivia replies:

> *Go thou and seek the crowner, and let him sit*
> *o' my coz; for he's in the third degree of drink,*
> *he's drowned: go, look after him.*
>
> (I, v, 142–44)

There can hardly be a healthy sexuality in a man who is linked to the crowner (coroner) and who is drowned in drink, especially in light of the fact that drinking to great excess would likely function to inhibit sexual desire anyway. Shakespeare is, I think, suggesting that Sir Toby's excessive drinking is in fact a substitute for a healthy sexuality. It is, however, healthy that Sir Toby, who is "come so early by this lethargy" (I, v, 131–32) of drunkenness, can joke about it heartily.

Following our introduction to Sir Toby in I, iii, our next extended meeting with him is in II, iii, the function of which is to initiate the plot to gull Malvolio. In broad terms the plot to gull—"sport royal" (186)—acts as a hold on the development of the character of Sir Toby. The scene repeats the previous emphasis on drinking and disorder and the soul-bearing banter of Maria and Sir Andrew is not resumed. The entrance of Malvolio, however, functions to create a developmental contrast between Malvolio and Sir Toby. The contrast is summed up in Sir Toby's oft quoted remark to Malvolio, "Dost thou think, because thou art virtuous, there shall be no more cakes and ale?" (123–24). Sir Andrew characterizes Malvolio as "a kind of puritan" (151), and Maria describes him as "so crammed as he thinks, with excellencies, that it is his grounds of faith that all that look on him love him" (162–64). Malvolio as puritan becomes a foil for Sir Toby as spokesman for a life that holds pleasure to be a good. Moreover, Malvolio as a man of vanity becomes a foil for those with the wit, intelligence, and worldliness to recognize vanity easily as a vice. In this way Shakespeare draws our attention from the worst implications of Sir Toby's character, and thus the comic point of view is distinctly maintained. But the rub is that Shakespeare has already initiated serious matter which the Malvolio-Sir Toby contrast illuminates.

Malvolio the puritan is a man of vanity and of repressed emotion, but we know that Sir Toby for all of his rhetorical protestations to the contrary is also a man ultimately in flight from himself. The scene therefore raises the question of what meaning the gulling of Malvolio will have in terms of the fundamental problems of Sir Toby's character, which is to say, his neurotic self which finds release for pent-up energies in drinking and jesting. The need to hatch a plot such as the one to gull Malvolio strongly implies the boredom that afflicts the lives of Sir Toby, Maria, and Sir Andrew. The opening of the scene, incidentally, anticipates this theme of boredom when Sir Andrew and Sir Toby demand a song of the Clown, who obliges with the beautiful, "O mistress mine." Sir Andrew and Sir Toby are, that is, always looking for some way to fill up their time. Shakespeare's technique is essentially to present us with farce counterpointed with provocative questions about character, but it is of the utmost importance that the questions are not mere repeats of what has been asked before.

The next scene involving Sir Toby, II, v, is one of the funniest scenes of the play, but Sir Toby is not at the center of the fun. The focus of the scene is, rather, on Malvolio's discovery of the letter, the letter itself—"be not afraid of greatness" (156)—and Malvolio's reaction to it. At the end of the scene, however, Sir Toby says, "Why, thou hast put him in such a dream, that when the image of it leave him he must run mad" (211–12). What Sir Toby means by "dream" clearly refers to Malvolio's vain image of himself. But in its way "sport royal" is also such a dream, if not a vain image of self at least an escape from self. The question is, do we *feel* this as we view one of the funniest scenes of the play. I think the answer is yes, in part because the idea of madness is introduced, and in the context of Sir Toby taking a genuine pleasure in Malvolio's pain. The madness which Sir Toby foresees as Malvolio's fate is, it seems to me, parallel to his own madness as a man in the third degree of drink, drowned. The counterpoint to the farcical hilarity of Malvolio's reaction to the letter is, then, vicious aggressiveness and intolerance. Olivia has accurately characterized Malvolio as "sick of self-love" (I, v, 97). Malvolio would reform people—and particularly Sir Toby—but this is not the same as taking pleasure in hurting them, which from the comic dramatist's point of view is madness.

In the next scene, III, i, we see Sir Toby only briefly; he is on stage for a mere twenty-seven lines, during which he encounters Viola, who is, of course, disguised as Cesario. The encounter is, however, highly significant, with this crucial exchange:

> Sir Toby: *Taste your legs, sir; put them to motion.*
> Viola: *My legs do better understand me, sir, than I understand what you mean by bidding me taste my legs.*
> Sir Toby: *I mean, to go, sir, to enter.*
>
> (88–92)

We can at this point fairly assume that Sir Toby means something lascivious, namely, to have carnal knowledge of (legs as a synecdoche), as well as the normal sense of to try or test. Since Viola is in fact a woman, it is likely that Sir Toby is expressing a sensual response to her, but since she is disguised as a man—not to mention played by a boy actor—a homosexual overtone is implied, which in turn might further explain why Sir Toby is what he is. His final remark is ambiguous. He is either, as part of his vulgar wit, advising Cesario to enjoy sexual relations since he seems sensually equipped to do so, or is suggesting his own homosexual intent toward Cesario. Such a revelation is an important increment in the development of the character of Sir Toby.

The revelation is followed in the very next scene, III, ii, by a confirmation of its content. Sir Toby busies himself gulling Sir Andrew into a duel with Cesario, expressing himself in terms that imply, it seems to me, the fierce aggressiveness of his sexuality:

> *Challenge me the count's youth to fight*
> *with him; hurt him in eleven places*   (36–7)

> *... as many lies as will lie in thy sheet of paper*
> *... set 'em down. . . . Let there be gall enough*
> *in thy ink . . .*   (49–52)

I take hurting Cesario "in eleven places" to be a lascivious reference to a sexual assault on the seven orifices of the human body plus the eyes and breasts and hence to imply that Sir Toby is depraved. It would, moreover, not be going too far to suggest that in this context gall in the ink refers to bitter and bitterly impersonal semen, that is, to sex as a human lie, with the vicarious sexual attack which Sir Toby is suggesting being homosexual anyway. But I do not think that in this instance Sir Toby is conscious of such a meaning, and it certainly must be said that this is the kind of comment that must be controlled with care lest the excesses of criticism become a substitute for an examination of the play. My own view is that Shakespeare is creating a telling irony, for Sir Toby is a man of intelligence and insight and yet is drowned in neurosis. Whereas Bottom is a victim and yet is free, Sir Toby is free and yet is a victim of himself. That Sir Toby for all of his intelligence does not perceive the full implication of what he himself says is the ironic point. He is not truly aware that he is a prisoner of his own sexuality, his own depravity. The scene as we view it is, of course, part of the farcical pattern of the play, with the gulling of Sir Andrew logical enough following the gulling of Malvolio, the results of which Maria describes at the end of the scene and which we are about to view in III, iv. Shakespeare is, it seems to me, quite deliberate in moving the play as farce as he counterpoints farce with meanings which if dwelled upon too long would terrify us and thus break the comic point of view of the play.

That Shakespeare intends to maintain the comic point of view is confirmed by his treatment of the action of the play in III, iv, a crucial scene involving the comedy of Malvolio as gull and Sir Toby's machinations to bring Sir Andrew into a fight with Cesario. The overall emphasis of the scene with regard to Sir Toby is that his plan will not work, which is to say, Shakespeare has brought his characterization of Sir Toby about as far as he intends and will now turn to resolution, as is appropriate to comedy. The most obvious symbol—for purposes of comedy—that Sir Toby's machinations are to

be held within the comic frame is the entrance of Antonio to rescue Viola-Cesario, whom he takes to be
Viola's twin brother Sebastian. Another indicator of
comic purpose is, of course, the fact that Sir Toby, not
knowing that Cesario is a woman, assumes that Cesario
will react with fury to Sir Andrew's challenge. Since
we know at all times that Viola is in disguise, our view
of Sir Toby is a view of the spectacle of his disappointed
expectation. Viola-Cesario responding to the challenge
is, moreover, a triumph of innocence, honesty, and
courtesy, that is, she is by definition unassailable; for
example, Sir Toby is the *victim* of the joke when with
his sword-as-phallus or sex-as-manliness wit he says to
Viola, "therefore, on, or strip your sword stark naked;
for meddle you must, that's certain, or forswear to wear
iron about you" (274–76). That the characterization
of Sir Toby will not be taken much further is also suggested by the fact that even Sir Toby has his limits; he
comments on Malvolio:

> *Come, we'll have him in a dark room and*
> *bound. My niece is already in the belief that*
> *he's mad: we may carry it thus, for our pleas-*
> *ure and his penance, till our very pastime, tired*
> *out of breath, prompt us to have mercy on him*
> (148–52)

Although Sir Toby's idea of mercy is far short of the
mercy of the comic spirit, he at least posits that his
sport has some limits, and there is at least a suggestion of
health in the idea that when the joke is exhausted life
will return to normal—in tragedy, by contrast, things

can never be anywhere near the same at the end as they were at the beginning. Moreover, since Sir Toby is clearly becoming a victim he is becoming an example of the comic-pathetic. His comment to Sir Andrew, "I'll ride your horse as well as I ride you" (317–18) is a metaphor of his sexual aggressiveness, and yet at this point we see him as rather harmless and ineffectual, which is Shakespeare's way, among many, of controlling the comic point of view.

Having made it clear that Sir Toby is to be viewed as comic-pathetic spectacle, Shakespeare turns next to the comedy of mistaken identity as, in IV, i, Sir Toby briefly encounters Sebastian, whom he takes to be Cesario and goads to swordplay. Against Sebastian Sir Toby presents himself as a ridiculous spectacle. Even his carnality—"Come, my young soldier, put up your iron: you are well fleshed; come on" (41–3)—takes on the aspect of the ridiculous rather than the provocative counterpoint to farce which we have seen.

The next scene, IV, ii, is Malvolio in a dark room— "they have laid me here in hideous darkness" (33–4). A question that has to be raised is whether or not this represents carrying a joke too far and thus exposing the dark side of life to the point at which comedy is no longer comedy. The answer to this question is, I think, negative, for two basic reasons. The first is the promise of mercy made by Sir Toby himself (III, iv, 152). The second is that Sir Toby has been rendered ineffectual and thus we do not experience the hideous darkness as a metaphor for the triumph of the element of depravity in the personality of Sir Toby. Moreover, Sir Toby, whom we more and more see as a natural coward, backs down: "I would we were well rid of this knavery . . . . for I am now so far in offence with my niece that I cannot pursue with any safety this sport to the upshot" (72–6). But with the mercy of the comic spirit in mind, it should be said that in his heart of hearts he probably does not wish to pursue the knavery. The scene, it seems to me, is very funny as farce, and its emphasis on madness is an emphasis on comic madness.

Once Sir Toby is established in III, iv, as a comic-pathetic spectacle, he has little further role in the play. Although present in the scene of Malvolio in a dark room, his participation in it is relatively minor. In the last act Sir Andrew first describes Sir Toby as having been given "a bloody coxcomb" (V, i, 179) by Sebastian and Sir Toby makes a brief final appearance, speaking only six lines. His bloody coxcomb is a final symbol of his comic-pathetic self, although Fabian later relates that he has married Maria. The two certainly deserve each other—and the announcement of their marriage emphasizes the comic point of view—and we are left to wonder what their lives together will be like, but theirs is not a love match and that tells us, I think, all we need to know.

We can imagine that as Sir Toby and Maria share a nuptial contemplation of one another that they hardly experience a dream in the sense of a vision, a perception of something beyond their own finitude. But what of Viola and Orsino, whose story begins and ends the play? As a heroine of comedy Viola is certainly closer in spirit to Rosalind than to Beatrice. Viola can, that is, sing beyond intellect. But is this enough to make *Twelfth Night* a comedy whose affirmation is less limited than the af-

firmation in *Much Ado About Nothing?* The answer to
this question is, I think, no, and for two basic reasons.
The first is that Viola lacks the commanding stature of
Rosalind. *Twelfth Night* is not Viola's play in the sense
that *As You Like It* is Rosalind's play. *Twelfth Night*
might have been Sir Toby's play but Shakespeare is
careful to use incremental development of his character
in order to render him, as it were, innocuous—not in
command of the play—whereas incremental development of character in Rosalind's case is for the very purpose of her dominating the play. The second reason why
Viola as heroine does not make *Twelfth Night* a comedy
whose affirmation is less limited than that of *Much Ado
About Nothing* may be found in the characterization of
Orsino. On the surface Orsino is an oddball sentimental-
ist, but his nature has another side. He is, for example,
the Duke whom Antonio has good reason to fear, and
in the last act his ferocity, as the other side of the coin
of sentimentality, manifests itself, particularly in his
angry response to the loss of Olivia to Cesario, addressed
to Olivia:

> *Why should I not, had I the heart to do it,*
> *Like to the Egyptian thief at point of death,*
> *Kill what I love?—a savage jealousy*
> *That sometime savours nobly. But hear me this:*
> *Since you to non-regardance cast my faith,*
> *And that I partly know the instrument*
> *That screws me from my true place in your*
> *   favour,*
> *Live you the marble-breasted tyrant still;*
> *But this your minion, whom I know you love,*

And whom, by heaven I swear, I tender dearly,
Him will I tear out of that cruel eye,
Where he sits crowned in his master's spite.
Come, boy, with me; my thoughts are ripe in
  mischief:
I'll sacrifice the lamb that I do love,
To spite a raven's heart within a dove.

(V, i, 120–34)

Since Cesario is really Viola there is no problem and
Orsino soon accepts Viola as his bride. But Shakespeare's
point, I think, is that Orsino is a man who sublimates his
strong sexual drive, first in sentimentality, as would-be
lover, and in the challenges of state, and finally, and
healthily—especially in light of the implication that his
anger implies a homosexual attraction to Cesario, "the
lamb that I do love"—in his marriage to Viola. This is,
I think, Shakespeare's wry and tolerant view of, his
joke about, Orsino, who is linked to Sir Toby, who tries
to sublimate his confused sexuality in sport, or jest. Thus
at the end of the play Sir Toby's excess is modified by
his marriage to Maria and Orsino is rescued from the
destructive potential of his excess by Viola's love. Viola's
lack of commanding stature and Orsino's psychological
make-up are tantamount to author insistence that the
world which we see at the end of *Twelfth Night* is not
a song beyond intellect, in fact not even a song that
could match that of Beatrice and Benedick in its lyric
strength.

It is significant that *Twelfth Night* is a comedy without a villain, without, that is, a character who is estranged
from his essential being. The presence of such a character

in comedy tells us that the author is able to see life in terms of fundamental values contrasts, able to see a world in which ethical values are clear-cut. But the world which Shakespeare calls Illyria, although values and ethics are clearly identifiable in it, is a world that in and of itself is moving in the direction of the values maelstrom of tragedy. Orsino, Sir Toby, and Malvolio are not men estranged from their essential being in the sense that sin is their choice, but they are also not men who will ever know the ultimate beauty of fellowship or the perfection of freedom.

Chapter Twelve

Shakespeare's Theory of Comedy, Fifth Statement

The answer to the question of what *Twelfth Night* adds to Shakespeare's theory of comedy may be seen as a paradox: it adds everything and yet nothing. The everything is, of course, all that *Twelfth Night* finally is and does as a comedy, particularly the way in which it takes the extremes of farce and psychological complexity and makes them complement one another. The nothing is that *Twelfth Night* does not add a plainly new ingredient to the recipe for comedy. In Viola in disguise we have the idea of courtship as imagination which we have seen in *The Taming of the Shrew, A Midsummer Night's Dream,* and *As You Like It* and to which *As You Like It* adds the idea of trial and error, or of self-discovery. There is, in my view, even less self-discovery in the Viola-Orsino courtship than in the courtship of Beatrice and Benedick, but, relative weights aside, the fact is that *Twelfth Night* makes distinct use of courtship as a motif —we could say an identifying device—of comedy and also of disguise to symbolize the trial-and-error process by which we come to knowledge of ourselves and of our world. *Twelfth Night* also makes conspicuous use of depth characterization as process, but unlike *As You Like It* concentrates this quality in the character of Sir Toby rather than in the lovers, Viola and Orsino. Similarly, *Twelfth Night* is a play whose wit has the tremendous appeal to intellect which we see in the wit of *Much Ado About Nothing*, but *Twelfth Night* concentrates this appeal not in the lovers but in the pranksters, Sir Toby, Maria, and Sir Andrew. Finally, *Twelfth Night* identifies itself strongly in terms of its lyricism, its songs being some of Shakespeare's best and its language more generally revealing the commanding lyricism which is an important if not a vital ingredient of comedy.

That Shakespeare was applying his theoretical understanding of comedy in *Twelfth Night* seems to me to be strongly suggested by the fact that *Twelfth Night* begins as a throwback to much earlier work. He was surely conscious of the fact that to take up the device of identical twins from Plautine comedy—a device which he had used in *The Comedy of Errors* and from which he had essentially turned away—was to challenge himself to reach for something new with something old and rather miserably mechanical. It is no surprise that as we view *Twelfth Night* we hardly feel that the device is too blatant or that the author is its captive. Shakespeare was also surely conscious of the fact that the hilarious farce of *Twelfth Night* was a return to the spirit of *The Taming of the Shrew*. It is, then, hard not to conclude that when he wrote *Twelfth Night* one of his principal concerns was to bring what he recognized as extremes into a right relationship. His basic technique in the play, farce counterpointed with provocative content, represents, in other words, the addition of something new to what for the sake of convenience I have been referring to as his theory of comedy. *Twelfth Night* is a comedy of provocative content, but since any good comedy is provocative in its content—develops, that is, a view of reality

—the provocative content of *Twelfth Night* must be regarded as a matter of degree. My own view is that the content of *Twelfth Night* is so provocative that Shakespeare *had* to deliver it in the medium of farce; more specifically, I think he was exploiting the speed and surfacyness of farce in order to draw attention away from provocative content and thus to maintain comic point of view. But speculation as to what Shakespeare had to do quickly threatens to become silly, especially insofar as it assumes a rational order in the creation of art, such as a choice of content, however provocative, followed by a choice of form, farce or whatever. Although I think that it is rational to suggest that Shakespeare had a theoretical understanding of what he was doing, to make such a suggestion is not the same as to say that he was following some kind of theory as he wrote. Let it suffice to say that he was an artist who concentrated his talents on the act of writing a play.

Chapter Thirteen

A Universe of Comedy

The purpose of the present study has been to present five of Shakespeare's comedies as an illustration of the fundamental working, the dynamics of Shakespearean comedy, with the hope that the five taken together have revealed a final unity which is distinctive in its kind. The essence of that unity is, it seems to me, that Shakespeare creates a universe of comedy, a world, or worlds, where the human spirit affirms itself and where values are there to make the affirmation possible. That universe is permeated by the comic spirit, which is a spirit of affirmation manifesting itself in many kinds of laughter, ranging from the hearty guffaws of farce, to the laughter both loud and quiet evoked by wit, to delight in the deep beauty of life, to that touch of a smile which is an exultation in human freedom, and to the peace that passes understanding. A given comedy may, of course, emphasize one or another kind of laughter, but the great comic dramatist has the skill to evoke them in a multiplicity of balances and combinations. It is in this way, I think, that Shakespeare as a comic dramatist is altogether faithful to the complexity of human experience. He never let a formula interfere with life.

143

Bibliographical Note

I refer specifically in my text to seven authors. The references here and there to Paul Tillich are all to the essay "Existential Analyses and Religious Symbols," which appears in *Contemporary Problems in Religion*, ed. Harold A. Basilius (Detroit: Wayne State University Press, 1956) and is conveniently available in the Anchor Book *Four Existentialist Theologians*, ed. Will Herberg (New York: Doubleday, 1958). A reading of the Tillich essay will provide, I think, a valuable philosophical orientation to the study of comedy. Henri Bergson's classic *Laughter* (1900) is also conveniently available in an Anchor Book, *Comedy*, ed. Wylie Sypher (New York: Doubleday, 1956), which includes another classic, George Meredith's *The Idea of Comedy and the Uses of the Comic Spirit* (1877). Bergson's ideas, which cut so well to fundamentals, are everywhere reflected in modern discussions of comedy. Maynard Mack's Introduction (1948) to the Rinehart Edition of Henry Fielding's *Joseph Andrews* provides not only interesting insights but also what to my mind is some of the most useful terminology for the study of comedy yet to appear. Samuel Johnson's "Preface to Shakespeare" (1765), with which every student of Shakespeare should be familiar, is conveniently available in the Rinehart Edition of his *Selected Prose and Poetry*, ed. Bertrand H. Bronson. Harold Goddard's excellent essay on *As You Like It* appears in *The Meaning of Shakespeare* (Chicago: University of Chicago Press, 1951), which also contains essays on the four other plays treated in the present study. All five essays are reprinted in volume I of the Phoenix Books edition (1960). Helen Gardner's essay " 'As You Like it' " appears in *More Talking of Shakespeare*, ed. John Garrett (New York: Theatre Arts Books, 1959) and is reprinted in *Modern Shakespearean Criticism: Essays on Style, Dramaturgy, and the Major Plays*, ed. Alvin B. Kernan (New York: Harcourt, Brace, and World, 1970). Finally, no student of comedy should fail to examine Sigmund Freud's *Jokes and Their Relation to the Unconscious* (1905), which is available in the James Strachey translation in the Norton Library edition (New York: W. W. Norton, 1963). Freud's psychoanalytic approach to jokes provides, I think, an interesting balance to the philosophical orientation to the study of comedy which may be had from a reading of Tillich.

For a general view of comedy, to be recommended is Northrop Frye's *Anatomy of Criticism: Four Essays* (Princeton: Princeton University Press, 1957), specifically the chapter "The Mythos of Spring: Comedy." Bernard M. Schilling's *The Comic Spirit: Boccaccio to Thomas Mann* (Detroit: Wayne State University Press, 1965) is an insightful series of essays, though none Shakespearean, on viewing the ludicrous sympathetically.

Some additional studies of interest are as follows:

Barber, C. L. *Shakespeare's Festive Comedy*. Princeton: Princeton University Press, 1959.

Brown, John Russell. *Shakespeare and His Comedies*. London: Methuen, 1957.

Charlton, H. B. *Shakespearean Comedy*. New York: Macmillan, 1938.

Evans, Bertrand. *Shakespeare's Comedies*. Oxford: Clarendon Press, 1960.

Leech, Clifford. *Twelfth Night and Shakespearean Comedy*. Halifax, N.S.: Dalhousie University Press, 1965.

Meader, William G. *Courtship in Shakespeare: Its Relation to the Tradition of Courtly Love*. New York: Columbia University Press, 1954.

Palmer, John. *Comic Characters of Shakespeare*. London: Macmillan, 1946.

Parrott, Thomas M. *Shakespearean Comedy*. New York: Oxford University Press, 1949.

Phialas, Peter G. *Shakespeare's Romantic Comedies: the Development of Their Form and Meaning*. Chapel Hill: University of North Carolina Press, 1966.

Prouty, Charles T. *The Sources of Much Ado About Nothing*. New Haven: Yale University Press, 1950.

Spurgeon, Caroline. *Shakespeare's Imagery and What It Tells Us*. New York: Macmillan, 1935.

Stoll, Elmer Edgar. *Shakespeare's Young Lovers*. New York: Oxford University Press, 1937.

Tillyard, E. M. W. *The Nature of Comedy and Shakespeare*. London: Oxford University Press, 1958.
Shakespeare's Early Comedies. New York: Barnes and Noble, 1965.

Vyvyan, John. *Shakespeare and Platonic Beauty*. New York: Barnes and Noble, 1961.

Wilson, John Dover. *Shakespeare's Happy Comedies*. London: Faber and Faber, 1962.

Young, David P. *Something of Great Constancy: the Art of A Midsummer Night's Dream*. New Haven: Yale University Press, 1966.